# CRITICAL ANALYSES
## IN
# ENGLISH RENAISSANCE DRAMA

*A Bibliographic Guide*

# Critical Analyses
## in
# English Renaissance Drama

## *A Bibliographic Guide*

# Brownell Salomon

Bowling Green University Popular Press
Bowling Green, Ohio 43403
for the
BGSU Center for Bibliography

Bowling Green University Popular Press
Bowling Green, Ohio 43403
for the
BGSU Center for Bibliography

Library of Congress Catalog Card Number: 78-70633
ISBN (cloth): 0-87972-127-8
      (paper): 0-87972-125-1

Cover illustration: title-page woodcut of Beaumont and Fletcher's *The Maid's Tragedy* (London, 1619; STC 1676), reproduced by permission of The Folger Shakespeare Library, Washington, D.C.

Ornaments: executed (probably) by Bernard Salomon, from the print shop of Jean de Tournes, Lyons, 1558. Reproduced from Albert Fidelis Butsch, *Handbook of Renaissance Ornament* (New York: Dover, 1969).

For Aubrey Williams,
with whom interpreting engaged
deeper, sharper insights

# CONTENTS

# PREFACE

This bibliographic guide directs the reader to a prize selection of the best modern, analytical studies of every play, anonymous play, masque, pageant, and "entertainment" written by more than two dozen contemporaries of Shakespeare in the years between 1580 and 1642. Together with Shakespeare's plays, these works comprise the most illustrious body of drama in the English language.

Intended as a practical reference work for the general reader and the undergraduate or graduate student enrolled in Elizabethan and Stuart drama courses, the Guide should also be a boon to the scholar-teacher, critic, and theatrical specialist. For the general reader it provides an effective handbook to the mass of criticism written on English Renaissance drama in the past half-century. Indeed, there is so much commentary, and a good deal of it of uneven quality or superseded by more recent studies, that it is no longer practicable for the general reader to examine all of it and judge for himself. But because some knowledge of modern approaches to this group of works is useful to even the most casual reader, the Guide would respond to that need. Students preparing a term paper or wishing to do independent reading will be assisted as never before. For them, locating the major booklength studies of an author or subject in the library card catalog is no problem; but discerning the leading practical criticism does require guidance. The scholar-teacher, critic, or graduate student will be able to use the Guide as a point of departure for wider research, for although its readings are highly selective, they are almost prerequisites to any new inquiry. These readers, too, will be afforded quick insight into which plays have already been well "mined" and which invite further interpretation. Theatrical specialists (and the growing number of commentators who see performance elements as inseparable from literary analysis) will find the Analytical Subject Index of special value, for it itemizes a wide range of theatrical data which the critics have judged relevant to their interpretations. Readers pursuing a full-scale research interest in the playwrights and their plays are advised to use the Guide in conjunction with its numerous sources, cited below.

Bibliographic items in the Guide's main section are arranged chronologically under the titles of the individual works, which are listed alphabetically after the dramatist's name. Performance dates are for the most part those assigned in Alfred Harbage, *Annals of English Drama, 975-1700,* rev. S. Schoenbaum (London: Methuen, 1964), and are used with the kind permission of Professor Schoenbaum. The only excluded categories of references are studies written in a language other than English, and unpublished theses and doctoral dissertations.

Two notable features which enhance the Guide's utility and distinguish it from other subject bibliographies of English Renaissance drama are as follows:

Every entry is annotated with a concise but informative summary of its content and critical approach.

The Analytical Subject Index is not simply an index to the Guide itself, but (taking its cue from the Subject Index of the *MLA Abstracts of Articles in Scholarly Journals* [1970-75]) is a thorough content and approach analysis of every critical item, intensively cross-referenced. For example, each significantly discussed theme, motif, and instance of thematic imagery or diction is detailed under "Themes."

Sources of the Guide were as comprehensive as possible, to lessen the chances of overlooking a qualified item. Mainstay was *The New Cambridge Bibliography of English Literature,* I (Cambridge: Cambridge Univ. Press, 1974), for which the Tudor and Stuart dramatic segments were compiled respectively by Professors G.R. Hibbard and Cyrus Hoy. Supplementing this resource were author and title entries in the *British Humanities Index, Essay and General Literature Index, MLA International Bibliography, Modern Humanities Research Association Annual Bibliography of English Language and Literature, Social Sciences and Humanities Index* (since 1974, the *Humanities Index*), and the "Renaissance Books" sections of *Renaissance Quarterly.* Though I accept full responsibility for including or excluding any item, I have sought out the well-regarded judgments of others, as expressed in the annual review articles entitled "Recent Studies in Elizabethan and Jacobean Drama" which appear in the spring number of *Studies in English Literature, 1500-1900,* and those which are a feature of *The Year's Work in English Studies.* Also consulted were volumes of a series of useful discursive bibliographies severally entitled *The Predecessors of Shakespeare* (1973) and *The Popular School* (1975), both bearing the subtitle *A Survey and Bibliography of Recent Studies in English Renaissance Drama,* eds. Terence P. Logan and Denzell S. Smith (Lincoln: Univ. of Nebraska Press, 1973—); and *Tudor and Stuart Drama* (Arlington Heights, Ill.: AHM, 1966), compiled by the late Irving Ribner for the Goldentree Bibliographies series. Heeded too were the selections of criticism in such major anthologies as *Elizabethan Drama: Modern Essays in Criticism,* ed. R.J. Kaufmann (New York: Oxford Univ. Press, 1961), and *Shakespeare's Contemporaries: Modern Studies in English Renaissance Drama,* eds. Max Bluestone and Norman Rabkin, 2nd ed. (Englewood Cliffs, N.J.: Prentice-Hall, 1970). Frieda Elaine Penninger's *English Drama to 1660 (Excluding Shakespeare): A Guide to Information Sources* (Detroit:

Gale Research Co., 1976) was of only limited value, for it excludes all criticism published in periodicals. Preparation of the section entitled Masques, Pageants, Entertainments was much facilitated by David M. Bergeron, *Twentieth-Century Criticism of English Masques, Pageants, and Entertainments: 1558-1642* (San Antonio, Tex.: Trinity Univ. Press, 1972).

Some statement is in order regarding the criteria used in selecting the analyses themselves. For an essay or autonomous portion of a book-length study to have qualified for inclusion in the Guide, one of its primary attributes had to be that it approached the dramatic work as a coherent unity rather than as an object of fragmentary or local interest. Expressed another way, the critical strategy employed by the commentator was required to be appropriate to the particular dramatic work, to bear significantly upon the work in its entirety, and to have concrete evidential support from the text. Criticism is doubtless most valuable being at one humane *and* systematic. In ideal terms, then, superior interpretations are those which provide intelligent, well-written, particularized, full readings of the play's meaning and impact, as determined by some notion of the *interdependence of theme, style, and structure.* By "theme" is meant the one or more abstract, all-infusing ideas or attitudes in a work—the cognitive or emotive concepts most fully and persistently alive to the dramatist as he was writing. By "style" is meant a play's texture, composed of both verbal data (language: as thematic imagery, diction, motifs, or rhetorical devices) and nonverbal, theatrical data (vocal tone, gesture, movement, make-up, costume, props, decor, lighting, music, and sound effects).[1] By "structure" is meant a play's architectonics, the significant unifying relations existing among scenes or episodes of the main plot and/or one or more subplots (produced by parallelism, juxtaposition, analogy, seriation, time-scheme, etc.); or existing as a complex of interaction or affinity among two or more characters; or existing as a pattern of symbolic actions formed around a mythopoeic or other deep-structural idea.[2] Theme, style, and structure together thus constitute three mutually reinforcing points of an "interpretation triangle." At the apex stands that flexible but quintessential factor, *theme,* which the critic derives from the literary text, clarifies perhaps with special knowledges, and offers as his own organizing perspective(s) on the work's overall unity of effect. As it is used here, however, theme is obliged to have specific textual referents, unlike the loose sense of the term that applies to paraphrasable literary topics or subject matter, as for instance one might speak of the "jealousy theme" in *Othello.* Thus, only when *theme* is concretely actualized in modes of *style* or *structure* (usually in both) does it acquire empirical bases for exact interpretive description.

Incidentally, with respect to its critical stance, the Guide is entirely pluralist: no "school" or approach—for examples, history of ideas, psychological criticism, exegesis of imagery, figural symbolism structuralism—is preferred over another, provided always that experience of the unique dramatic work, in and for itself and for its *dianoia* or meaning, is the primary concern and not simply the means to a different end. Items designated as "superior interpretations" are preceded by an identifying asterisk (*).

For the benefit of future editions of the Guide, I should be appreciative to hear of any errors which the reader may discover, and to receive suggestions for additions. The *MLA Directory* lists my academic address.

With pleasure I acknowledge the assistance given me in bringing this work to completion. I am grateful for the Special Achievement Award for Scholarship from President Hollis A. Moore and the Board of Trustees of Bowling Green State University, which carried a stipend that enabled me to do resident research at the Henry E. Huntington Library in December 1975. To the Faculty Research Committee I am obliged for a Part-time Research Associateship that same year, which defrayed ongoing expenses. At the Huntington, I valued the scholarly camaraderie and the kindnesses, in particular, of Virginia J. Renner and Noelle Jackson. My heartiest thanks go to Gloria Gregor, in charge of administrative services at the Bowling Green State University Library, who flattened the mountain of criticism I so much enjoyed reading into a manageable hill of xerographic copies. But for the Xerox machine, which also allowed most items to be put on file for constant comparisons and reevaluation, I would probably not have attempted this project on so wide a scale.

Bowling Green, Ohio
June 1977

[1]These eleven semiological categories (within the parentheses) appear as headings in the Analytical Subject Index.

[2]As with style, every such element or concept of structure, when it is pertinent to a critic's analysis, is recorded in the Analytical Subject Index, s.v. Structure, Archetypal criticism, etc. Indeed, many entries are there indexed or cross-referenced under more than two-dozen different content-analysis descriptors.

# Table of Abbreviations

| | |
|---|---|
| *Anglia* | Anglia: Zeitschrift für Englische Philologie |
| *AUMLA* | Journal of the Australasian Universities Language and Literature Association |
| *BJRL* | Bulletin of the John Rylands Library |
| *BSUF* | Ball State University Forum |
| *BUSE* | Boston University Studies in English |
| *CLAJ* | College Language Association Journal (Morgan State College, Baltimore) |
| *CompD* | Comparative Drama |
| *Criterion* (London) | |
| *Criticism* (Wayne State) | |
| *CritQ* | Critical Quarterly |
| *DramS* | Drama Survey (Minneapolis) |
| *DUJ* | Durham University Journal |
| *E&S* | Essays and Studies by Members of the English Association |
| *EIC* | Essays in Criticism (Oxford) |
| *ELH* | Journal of English Literary History |
| ElizS | Elizabethan & Renaissance Studies (University of Salzburg, Austria) |
| *ELR* | English Literary Renaissance |
| *EM* | English Miscellany |
| *English* (London) | |
| ES | English Studies |
| ESA | English Studies in Africa (Johannesburg) |
| *ETJ* | Educational Theatre Journal |
| *Genre* (State University of New York College at Plattsburgh) | |
| HAB | Humanities Association Bulletin (Canada) |
| HAR | Humanities Association Review (Canada)[Formerly *Humanities Association Bulletin*] |
| *HLQ* | Huntington Library Quarterly |
| *HussonR* | Husson Review |
| JDS | Jacobean Drama Studies (University of Salzburg, Austria) |
| *JEGP* | Journal of English and Germanic Philology |
| *JMRS* | Journal of Medieval and Renaissance Studies |
| *JWCI* | Journal of the Warburg and Courtauld Institute |
| *Komos: A Quarterly of Drama and Arts of the Theatre* | |
| *L&P* | Literature and Psychology (Fairleigh Dickinson University) |
| LSE | Lund Studies in English |
| *M&L* | Music and Letters (London) |
| *MHRev* | Malahat Review |
| *MLN* | Modern Language Notes (Baltimore) |
| *MLQ* | Modern Language Quarterly (Seattle) |
| *MLR* | Modern Language Review |
| *MP* | Modern Philology (Chicago) |
| *N&Q* | Notes and Queries |
| *Neophil* | Neophilologus (Groningen) |
| NM | Neuphilologische Mitteilungen |

| | |
|---|---|
| *PCP* | Pacific Coast Philology |
| *PLL* | Papers on Language and Literature |
| *PMLA: Publications of the Mod. Lang. Assn. of America* | |
| *PQ* | Philological Quarterly (Iowa City) |
| *QRL* | Quarterly Review of Literature (Bard College) |
| *REL* | Review of English Literature |
| *Ren&R* | Renaissance and Reformation |
| *RenD* | Renaissance Drama (Northwestern U.) |
| *RenP* | Renaissance Papers |
| *RES* | Review of English Studies |
| *RMS* | Renaissance & Modern Studies (University of Nottingham) |
| RRDS | Regents Renaissance Drama Series |
| *SAB* | South Atlantic Bulletin |
| *Scrutiny* (Cambridge) | |
| *SEL* | Studies in English Literature, 1500-1900 |
| SEngL | Studies in English Literature (The Hague) |
| *SFQ* | Southern Folklore Quarterly |
| *ShS* | Shakespeare Survey |
| *SP* | Studies in Philology |
| *TDR* | The Drama Review [Formerly *Tulane Drama Review*] |
| TEAS | Twayne's English Author Series |
| *ThR* | Theatre Research (London) |
| *Trivium* (St. David's College, Lampeter, Cardiganshire, Wales) | |
| *TSE* | Tulane Studies in English |
| *TSL* | Tennessee Studies in Literature |
| *TSLL* | Texas Studies in Literature and Language |
| *UTQ* | University of Toronto Quarterly |
| *XUS* | Xavier University Studies (New Orleans) |
| *YES* | Yearbook of English Studies |

# Critical Theory

1    EMPSON, William. *Seven Types of Ambiguity*. 2nd rev. ed. New York: New Directions, 1947; 1st ed. 1930. ["Ambiguity," either as polysemy or syntactical/grammatical complexity, is among the roots of literature. Of this bellwether of analytical criticism Stanley Hyman said in *The Armed Vision* (New York, 1948), "page after page contains the most elaborate and probably the finest close reading of poetry ever put down."]

2    FERGUSSON, Francis. *The Idea of a Theater: A Study of Ten Plays, The Art of Drama in Changing Perspective*. Princeton: Princeton Univ. Press, 1949. Pp. 98-142. [Aristotle's notion of analogous actions clarifies holistically *Hamlet*'s multiple plot, ritual patterns, etc.; thus, unity is expressible in terms of theme—a play's "supreme analogue"—using formal rather than lexical proofs. (In this Guide, instances are indexed s.v. Structure: interplot unifying concepts.)]

3    KNIGHT, G. Wilson. "On the Principles of Shakespeare Interpretation." *The Wheel of Fire: Interpretations of Shakespearian Tragedy*. 4th rev. ed. London: Methuen, 1949; 1st ed. 1930. Pp. 1-16. [Rarely has one critic exerted so profound an influence on dramatic studies. Eschewing to treat characters as rigid "particles," his field-theory approach to interpretation involves symbolic patters built organically around a thematic core,

and profuse documentation.]

4       DORAN, Madeleine. *Endeavors of Art: A Study of Form in Elizabethan Drama.* Madison: Univ. of Wisconsin Press, 1954. [This paragon of historical criticism examines the generic influences (e.g., *de casibus* tragedy, Roman comedy) and Renaissance assumptions about imitation, decorum, multiple unity, plotting, rhetoric, character, etc., which influence dramatic form and meaning.]

5       BARBER, C.L. *Shakespeare's Festive Comedy: A Study of Dramatic Form and Its Relation to Social Custom.* Princeton: Princeton Univ. Press, 1959. [The saturnalian pattern of Elizabethan sports and festive holidays, whereby revelry and mockery release inhibition and clarify man's relation to nature, is reflected in Shakespearean form and meaning—a most influential anthropological-psychological study.]

6       FRYE, Northrop. "Myth, Fiction, and Displacement" (1961). *Fables of Identity: Studies in Poetic Mythology.* New York: Harcourt, 1963. Pp. 21-38. [The influential discussions of genres, conventions, and archetypes in the *Anatomy of Criticism* (1957) are continued. Sees the abstract story-pattern of myth as the analyzable formal cause unifying all literature; displacement is mythic form reconciled with plausibility, lifelikeness.]

7       LEVIN, Richard. *The Multiple Plot in English Renaissance Drama.* Chicago: Univ. of Chicago Press, 1971. Pp. 1-20. [A brilliantly realized methodology (with debts to the Chicago neo-Aristotelians) for analyzing the ways in which multiple-plot actions are related or unified. Terms from Aristotle's *Physics* are used for such structural interconnections as direct linkage, parallelism and contrast, etc.]

8       ROSE, Mark. *Shakespearean Design.* Cambridge, MA: Harvard Univ. Press, 1972. [Approaches the inseparability of form and meaning in so integrative a way that all drama of the period should

be illuminated. Renaissance aesthetic notions of multiple unity and symmetrical proportion firmly ground discussions of such spatiotemporal patterns as diptych scenes, frame scenes, scenic parallelisms and groupings, and liaisons between scenes.]

9      SALOMON, Brownell. "Visual and Aural Signs in the Performed English Renaissance Play." *RenD*, N.S. 5 (1972), 143-69. [A play's meaning lies not only in its language but in nonverbal elements like vocal tone, gesture, movement, make-up, costume, hand properties, the decor, lighting, music, and sound effects. Semiology, the science of signs, aids interpretation by helping to organize a thematic gestalt from the work's diverse linguistic/presentational data.]

10     WETHERILL, P.M. *The Literary Text: An Examination of Critical Methods*. Berkeley: Univ. of California Press, 1974. [Superlatives are in order, for there is no fuller description of the aims, concepts, and tools (linguistics, semantics, computerization, etc.) of modern close analysis. An exponent of the Anglo-American school of practical criticism, the author champions the text *as literature*. In effect, the work details the critical assumptions behind this Guide.]

---

**Notes and Additions**

# Concordances & Word Indexes

## GEORGE CHAPMAN

**11** STAGG, Louis Charles. *An Index to the Figurative Language of George Chapman's Tragedies.* Charlottesville: Bibliographical Society of the Univ. of Virginia, 1970. [This 143-page booklet facilitates study of *Bussy D'Ambois; The Revenge of Bussy D'Ambois; Chabot, Admiral of France; Byron's Conspiracy; Byron's Conspiracy; Byron's Tragedy;* and *Caesar and Pompey.*]

## THOMAS HEYWOOD

**12** STAGG, Louis Charles. *An Index to the Figurative Language of Thomas Heywood's Tragedies.* Charlottesville: Bibliographical Society of the Univ. of Virginia, 1967. [This 54-page pamphlet will aid study of *1 & 2 Edward IV, The Rape of Lucrece,* and *A Woman Killed with Kindness;* lists key words alphabetically and by the categories of C. Spurgeon's *Shakespeare's Imagery* (1936).]

## BEN JONSON

13     STAGG, Louis Charles. *Index to the Figurative Language of Ben Jonson's Tragedies.* Charlottesville: Bibliographical Society of the Univ. of Virginia, 1967. [Until superseded by a comprehensive concordance, this 47-page pamphlet will aid study of *Sejanus His Fall* and *Catiline His Conspiracy;* lists key words alphabetically and by the categories of C. Spurgeon's *Shakespeare's Imagery* (1936).]

# THOMAS KYD

14     CRAWFORD, Charles, comp. *A Concordance to the Works of Thomas Kyd. Materialien zur kunde des alteren Englishchen Dramas.* Ed. W. Bang. Ser. 1, Vol. 15. 1906-10; rpt. Vaduz: Kraus, 1963. [This early concordance treats all plays which might have been written by Kyd: *The Spanish Tragedy* and its Additions, *Cornelia, Soliman and Perseda, 1 Jeronimo*—even *Arden of Feversham.* Today only the first two are confidently assigned to Kyd.]

# CHRISTOPHER MARLOWE

15     CRAWFORD, Charles, comp. *The Marlowe Concordance. Materialien zur Kunde des alteren Englishchen Dramas.* Ed. W. Bang and Henry De Vocht. Ser. 1, Vol. 34; Ser. 2, Vols. 3, 6-7, in 2 vols. 1911, 1929; rpt. Vaduz: Kraus, 1963. [The anonymous plays, *Edward III, Locrine,* and *1 Selimus,* are concorded in addition to Marlowe's works, ensuring long-lived utility for this work.]

# JOHN MARSTON

16     STAGG, Louis Charles. *An Index to the Figurative Language of*

Notes and Additions

*John Marston's Tragedies.* Charlottesville: Bibliographical Society of the Univ. of Virginia, 1970. [This 86-page index will aid study of *Antonio's Revenge, Sophonisba,* and *The Insatiate Countess* (tragic plot only); lists key words alphabetically and by the categories (war, sickness, etc.) of C. Sprugeon's *Shakespeare's Imagery.*]

# THOMAS MIDDLETON

17  STAGG, Louis Charles. *An Index to the Figurative Language of Thomas Middleton's Tragedies.* Charlottesville: Bibliographical Society of the Univ. of Virginia, 1970. [This 65-page pamphlet will aid study of *The Changeling* and *Women Beware Women;* lists key words alphabetically and by the categories of C. Sprugeon's *Shakespeare's Imagery* (1936).]

# JOHN MILTON (1608-1674)

18  INGRAM, William, and Kathleen SWAIN, [comps. and] eds. *A Concordance to Milton's English Poetry.* Oxford: Clarendon, 1972. [A computer-generated concordance to John Milton's *Comus* and his entertainment, *Arcades* (fragment). Unprinted lines of *Comus* from the Trinity and Bridgewater MSS. are given separate entries.]

# CYRIL TOURNEUR

19  STAGG, Louis Charles. *An Index to the Figurative Language of Cyril Tourneur's Tragedies.* Charlottesville: Bibliographical Society of the Univ. of Virginia, 1970. [Not a concordance, but a useful, 44-page index to *The Revenger's Tragedy* and *The Atheist's Tragedy;* lists key words alphabetically and by the categories of C.

Spurgeon's *Shakespeare's Imagery and What It Tells Us* (1936).]

# JOHN WEBSTER

**20** STAGG, Louis Charles. *An Index to the Figurative Language of John Webster's Tragedies.* Charlottesville: Bibliographical Society of the Univ. of Virginia, 1967. [Until superseded by a comprehensive concordance, this 58-page pamphlet, one of seven of its kind, will aid study of *The Duchess of Malfi, The White Devil,* and *Appius and Virginia*; lists key words alphabetically and by the categories (animals, etc.) of C. Spurgeon's Shakespeare's Imagery (1936).]

# Dramatists, 1580 - 1642,
# Excluding Shakespeare

## Francis Beaumont & John Fletcher

*A King and No King* (1611)

21    *MIZENER, Arthur. "The High Design of *A King and No King.*"
      *MP,* 38 (1940), 133-54. [Acts and scenes are ordered in terms of the
      primacy of "emotional or psychological form" (the complex, varied,
      and patterned sequence of feelings and effective attitudes to be
      stimulated in an audience), not in terms of a narrative form that is
      morally significant.]

22    WAITH, Eugene M. *The Pattern of Tragicomedy in Beaumont and
      Fletcher.* New Haven, CT: Yale Univ. Press, 1952. Pp. 27-42.
      [Defines eight formal characteristics of Beaumont and Fletcher's
      tragicomedy, which are finally and completely established with *A
      King and No King.* Notes the contrast between sexual depravity
      and ideal love.]

23    *TURNER, Robert K., Jr. "The Morality of *A King and No King.*"
      *RenP* (1960), 93-103. [Externalizing the raging conflict of Will and
      Reason within Arbaces, Mardonius functions as the Good Angel
      and Bessus plays a dual role as Vice and parodic alter ego of
      Arbaces. Arbaces' alteration is traced imagistically as he regresses
      from hero-king to man to beast.]

---

**Notes and Additions**

*The Knight of the Burning Pestle* (F. Beaumont alone; 1607)

24      DOEBLER, John. "Beaumont's *The Knight of the Burning Pestle*
        and the Prodigal Son Plays." *SEL,* 5 (1965), 333-44. [Beaumont
        satirizes middle-class morality by parodying its stock formal
        exemplars: Prodigal Son plays like *Nice Wanton* (1560) and
        *Misogonus* (ca. 1570), which derive from the moralities and from
        plays by the humanist Christianizers of Terence.]

25      *COPE, Jackson I. *The Theater and the Dream: From Metaphor to
        Form in Renaissance Drama.* Baltimore: Johns Hopkins Univ.
        Press, 1973. Pp. 196-210. [Folk festivity comprises the play's
        surface and substructure: Merrythought presides as Lord of
        Misrule over a spring celebration which sees Rafe and Jasper
        "revive" from death.]

*The Loyal Subject* (J. Fletcher alone; 1618)

26      WAITH, Eugene M. *The Pattern of Tragicomedy in Beaumont and
        Fletcher.* New Haven: Yale Univ. Press, 1952. Pp. 143-51. [Both
        plots involve variations on the conflict between honor and
        materialism, Archas and his family embodying the former trait,
        and the greedy, sensual Boroskie the latter. Sources in Bandello
        and Heywood are much altered.]

*The Mad Lover* (J. Fletcher alone; 1617)

27      GOSSETT, Suzanne. "Masque Influence on the Dramaturgy of
        Beaumont and Fletcher." *MP,* 69 (1972), 199-208. [For the
        playwrights, masques and their elements created self-aware shifts
        from real to unreal, or upset comic or tragic expectations; here, a
        thematically relevant fictive masque, with a bestial antimasque, is
        followed by a *real* theophany.]

*The Maid in the Mill* (J. Fletcher with W. Rowley; 1623)

---

**Notes and Additions**

28     *STEIGER, Klaus Peter. " 'May a Man be Caught with Faces?': The
       Convention of 'Heart' and 'Face' in Fletcher and Rowley's *The
       Maid in the Mill." E&S,* 20 (1967), 47-63. [Blind Cupid, in the play-
       within-the-play, is the central symbol. The difficulty in recognizing
       love is figured by metaphors of appearance (eye, face, outward
       beauty, blindness) and reality (heart, breast), and multiple
       disguises.]

## The Maid's Tragedy (ca. 1608-1611)

29     DANBY, John F. *Poets on Fortune's Hill: Studies in Sidney,
       Shakespeare, Beaumont and Fletcher.* London: Faber, 1952. Pp.
       152-206. [Finds the central interest not character, but radically
       dislocated, incongruous situations that wittily exploit contending
       absolutes such as love and duty. Petrarchan situations are
       punningly inverted.]

30     *ORNSTEIN, Robert. *The Moral Vision of Jacobean Tragedy.*
       Madison: Univ. of Wisconsin Press, 1960. Pp. 174-79. [Supplies
       interesting Freudian explications in keeping with the vein of
       morbidity said to underlie most of the play's action; e.g., Evadne's
       dagger thrusts during the regicide, like Melantius' drawn sword in
       IV.i, is phallic symbolism.]

31     GURR, Andrew, ed. *The Maid's Tragedy.* Fountainwell Drama Ser.
       Berkeley: Univ. of California Press, 1969. Pp. 2-6. [" 'Honour' is the
       key concept of the play, applied in one form or other more than forty
       times" (p. 5). Of the two main contemporary meanings of that word
       and "honesty," the playwrights stress personal reputation rather
       than virtue.]

32     *NEILL, Michael. " 'The Simetry, Which Gives a Poem Grace':
       Masque, Imagery, and the Fancy of *The Maid's Tragedy." RenD,*
       N.S. 3 (1970), 111-35. [A splendid, perceptive "total reading";
       analyzes the wedding masque (I.ii) as the structural and rhetorical
       center of the play's symmetry of inversions, perversions, and

peripeties. Examines thematic imagery in detail.]

*Philaster* (1609-1610)

33    *DANBY, John F. *Poets on Fortune's Hill: Studies in Sidney, Shakespeare, Beaumont and Fletcher.* London: Faber, 1952. Pp. 162-83. [Typically with Beaumont and Fletcher, the form of the play is dominated by *situational* conceits: willful, hyperbolic, either-or, Petrarchan conflicts of absolutes, such as love and duty.]

34    *GURR, Andrew, ed. *Philaster.* Revels Plays. London: Methuen, 1969. Pp. xlv-lxxi. [Comments upon the ways in which "service" and "servant" are key words in the play: in addition to the heroic sense (duty to lord or king), there are the amatorious and sexual ones. For Bellario, true service defines the concept of selfhood.]

*Rule a Wife and Have a Wife* (J. Fletcher alone; 1624)

35    LEVIN, Richard. *The Multiple Plot in English Renaissance Drama.* Chicago: Univ. of Chicago Press, 1971. Pp. 51-54. [Summarizes the play as one of the clearest examples of the direct-contrast structure: equivalent "wars of marriage," sexes transposed, in which the main-plot hero and subplot heroine dupe prospective mates by clever misrepresentation.]

*The Woman Hater* (1606)

36    *LEVIN, Richard. *The Multiple Plot in English Renaissance Drama.* Chicago: Univ. of Chicago Press, 1971. Pp. 151-54. [Structural unity is achieved through a direct contrast of extremes. The misogynist of the main plot and the gourmand of the parodic subplot are given homologous roles, equatable in their departure from the natural sexual norm.]

# Richard Brome

## The Antipodes (1638)

37      *DONALDSON, Ian. The World Upside-Down: Comedy from Jonson to Fielding. Oxford: Clarendon, 1970. Pp. 78-98. [For its central symbol and unifying idea *The Antipodes* takes a familiar geographic cenceit, the notion that sub-Equatorial manners and morals are an upside-down version of London's; as a result, diverse "madnesses" undergo a comic catharsis.]

38      *COPE, Jackson I. *The Theater and the Dream: From Metaphor to Form in Renaissance Drama*. Baltimore: Johns Hopkins Univ. Press, 1973. Pp. 143-59. [The paradoxical "reality" of an extemporal play-within-the-play mirrors an imaginative ideal, inverting reality according to Antipodean logic and restoring it as a norm.]

## The Damoiselle (1637-1638?)

39      *KAUFMANN, R.J. *Richard Brome, Caroline Playwright*. New York: Columbia Univ. Press, 1961. Pp. 131-50. [Vermine the usurer becomes a scapegoat figure ȯn whom society can direct resentment against misused wealth, for the cash-nexus is inimical to the Christian ideal of brotherhood which the play depicts in the relations of parents to children, men to men.]

## A Jovial Crew (1641)

40      *COPE, Jackson I. *The Theater and the Dream: From Metaphor to Form in Renaissance Drama*. Baltimore: Johns Hopkins Univ. Press, 1973. Pp. 159-69. [An anthropological interpretation: for the restraints of societal imprisonment, the liberty of "naturalness" and the natural forces of regeneration are proved the right correctives.]

## The Queen and Concubine (1635-1639)

41      *KAUFMANN, R.J. *Richard Brome, Caroline Playwright*. New

York: Columbia Univ. Press, 1961. Pp. 88-108. [A parabolic tragicomedy with technical affinities to Shakespeare's *Tempest,* the work is built upon interlocked contrasts in theme, character, and situation: court/country, passion/reason, light/dark, death/rebirth, and above all appearance/reality.]

42    COPE, Jackson I. *The Theater and the Dream: From Metaphor to Form in Renaissance Drama.* Baltimore: Johns Hopkins Univ. Press, 1973. Pp. 282-84, n. 64. [Merely an extended footnote to prove Brome's reliance upon Chapman's *Gentleman Usher* for centering his action upon providential "patience," but it supplies a micro-essay on the *felix culpa* theme.]

## *The Queen's Exchange* (1629-1632?)

43    COPE, Jackson I. *The Theater and the Dream: From Metaphor to Form in Renaissance Drama.* Baltimore: Johns Hopkins Univ. Press, 1973. Pp. 134-40. [A suggestive orientation into Brome's first experiment with the "pretended-prince" theme: prophetic dream-vision becomes reality when a look-alike commoner accepts the disguise and *becomes* king.]

## *The Weeding of the Covent Garden* (1632)

44    *KAUFMANN, R.J. *Richard Brome, Caroline Playwright.* New York: Columbia Univ. Press, 1961. Pp. 67-87. [Not propaganda, the play is yet "socially-orientated art"—forensic, reportorial as to current events and abuses, and topically satirical regarding Puritans. Familial paternalism is the subject, but ecclesio-political paternalism can be inferred.]

# George Chapman

*Bussy D'Ambois* (1600-1604)

45     *BARBER, C.L. "The Ambivalence of *Bussy D'Ambois.*" *REL*, 2
       (1961), 38-44. [*Bussy* anticipates later seventeenth-century heroic
       drama, which helps to explain its Restoration popularity and its
       unreconciled ambivalence: Bussy's duelling and adultery flout
       Christian morality (*blood* is a key word); yet this Man of Honor
       sympathetically defends the private code.]

46     RIBNER, Irving. *Jacobean Tragedy: The Quest for Moral Order.*
       New York: Barnes & Noble, 1962. Pp. 19-35. [Characters perform
       thematic functions within a didactic scheme. Bussy is an
       Everyman, the symbol of ordinary humanity vulnerable to
       society's corruption; but he also figures natural man in all the
       prelapsarian perfection of the "golden age."]

47     WAITH, Eugene M. *The Herculean Hero in Marlowe, Chapman,
       Shakespeare and Dryden.* New York: Columbia Univ. Press, 1962.
       Pp. 88-111. ["Purity of motive and corruption of act are brought out
       by the ambiguity of every major incident" (p. 111). Bussy is
       culpable, but occult nuances of darkness enhance a Herculean
       stature; Tamyra is similarly ambivalent.]

48     *BROOKE, Nicholas, ed. *Bussy D'Ambois.* Revels Plays. London:
       Metheun, 1964. Pp. xxvi-liv. [Analyzes dramatic poetry, structure,
       characterological aspects, and abstract/concrete emblematic
       staging to indicate the equivocal balances in the play—mankind as
       alternately heroic and antiheroic, free and determinate, admirable
       and self-deceiving.]

49     *BEMENT, Peter. "The Imagery of Darkness and of Light in
       Chapman's *Bussy D'Ambois.*" *SP*, 64 (1967), 187-98. [Imagery of
       darkness and light, whose import derives from a mystical
       Neoplatonic tradition, is structurally meaningful; daylight (active,
       passional life) is opposed by night (contemplative life). But after
       Act I, night symbolizes chaos.]

50     *WADDINGTON, Raymond B. *The Mind's Empire: Myth and Form
       in George Chapman's Narrative Poems.* Baltimore: Johns Hopkins

Univ. Press, 1974. Pp. 19-44. [Allusions establish a Hesiodic background, providing mythological correspondence for Bussy (Prometheus, Hercules), Tamyra (Pandora), and Bussy's *alter ego,* Monsieur. *Concordia discors* defines mythic form.]

## Caesar and Pompey (1599-1607)

51    *SCHWARTZ, Elias. "A Neglected Play by Chapman." *SP,* 58 (1961), 140-59. [Two movements are counterpointed in this structurally unified play: Caesar's self-exalting drive towards Roman conquest, and Cato's heroic attempt to counter Caesar; Pompey, rather than Cato, is the true tragic protagonist whose inner struggle mirrors the central conflict.]

52    CRAWLEY, Derek. "Decision and Character in Chapman's *The Tragedy of Caesar and Pompey." SEL,* 7 (1967), 277-97. [The main characters are differentiated, favorably or unfavorably, chiefly in terms of Stoic doctrine; Cato is perfect in that ethos, and though physically absent from II.iv to IV.v, remains the touchstone of personal and social worth.]

## The Conspiracy and Tragedy of Charles Duke of Byron (1608)
## i. Byron's Conspiracy (Part I)

53    *URE, Peter. "The Main Outline of Chapman's Byron." *SP,* 47 (1950), 568-88. [In Byron Plutarchan virtue wages a losing debate with fortune. There is no ethical ambiguity, for a dialectical scheme gives us a "dramatic," shifting view of him—as both a heroic, Alexander figure and one too susceptible to the vices of flattery, ambition, and megalomania.]

54    SCHWARTZ, Elias. "Chapman's Renaissance Man: Byron Reconsidered." *JEGP,* 58 (1959), 613-26. [Byron's immense, passionate, and self-exalting egotism is at the core of the play, for the lie of this self-deception creates the ironic perspective by which Byron's Machiavellian principles and quasi-divine sense of selfhood are implicitly condemned.]

55      MacLURE, Millar. *George Chapman: A Critical Study*. Toronto:
        Univ. of Toronto Press, 1966. Pp. 132-44. [While both parts of the
        play are treated at once here, MacLure stresses metaphors in *The
        Conspiracy* that define Byron's character as one of Herculean,
        humorous pride: "bursts," "blown up," "puff'd with...empty
        breath," "hot, shining, swift."]

56      STAGG, Louis Charles. "Characterization Through Nature
        Imagery in the Tragedies of George Chapman." *BSUF*, 9 (1968), 39-
        43. [Imagery of water and streams have especial potency in the
        play; discussion is brief (pp. 42-43), but the examples, such as
        billows smashing over rocks, lend insight into Byron's heroic
        stature as well as his presumptuousness.]

## ii. *Byron's Tragedy* (Part II)

57      *URE, Peter. "The Main Outline of Chapman's Byron." *SP*, 47
        (1950), 568-88. [King Henry emerges as the play's real Alexander, a
        wise prince whose ascension in political and ethical terms crosses
        Byron's fall, the result of Machiavellian corruption of virtue.
        Morality satisfied, the dying traitor claims our sympathy through
        religious poetic symbolism.]

58      SCHWARTZ, Elias. "Chapman's Renaissance Man: Byron
        Reconsidered." *JEGP*, 58 (1959), 613-26. [His evil assertion of
        selfhood eventuating in a death sentence for treason, Byron
        maintains his inviolate will against ego-crushing resignation; even
        death itself would be transcended. In the intentionally ambiguous
        final lines, victory is ironic, Pyrrhic.]

59      MacLURE, Millar. *George Chapman: A Critical Study*. Toronto:
        Univ. of Toronto Press, 1966. Pp. 132-44. [Byron of Part II is the
        same man as before, but now his atheism (I.iii.4-6) and likeness to
        powerless animals is emphasized; by contrast, King Henry, the
        exemplar of order, is a sun-king (e.g., V.i.138-46) who appears in a
        new religious aspect.]

**Notes and Additions**

**60**     STAGG, Louis Charles. "Characterization Through Nature
Imagery in the Tragedies of George Chapman." *BSUF,* 9 (1968), 39-
43. [A single page (p. 43) is devoted to this play, but it points out
numerous metaphors consciously drawn from external nature,
observing that "violent weather images keep pace with the
increased violence of Byron's temper."]

**61**     HOMAN, Sidney R. "Chapman and Marlowe: The Paradoxical
Hero and the Divided Response." *JEGP,* 68 (1969), 391-406.
[Conscious dramatic technique accounts for Byron's "impossible
mixtures" (V.iii.190): the strong warrior—"valor," meaning *virtu,*
echoes throughout—is also a deluded egoist. As antithesis, the king
is just, merciful, but flatly expedient.]

## *Eastward Ho* (with B. Jonson & J. Marston; 1605)

**62**     HORWICH, Richard. "*Hamlet* and *Eastward Ho.*" *SEL,* 11 (1971),
223-33. [*Eastward Ho* imitates and parodies *Hamlet*: there are the
same oppositions of reason and passion, of thrift and prodigality
(as psychological and economic traits), and many thematic echoes;
irony is produced by disparities of seriousness and complexity
between the plays.]

**63**     LEVIN, Richard. *The Multiple Plot in English Renaissance
Drama.* Chicago: Univ. of Chicago Press, 1971. Pp. 88-89. [Sketches
this comedy's three-level structural design, which hearkens back to
*Damon and Pythias* and *Nice Wanton* and involves a "hierarchy of
moral, immoral, and amoral actions presented in the three modes of
decreasing seriousness."]

**64**     *COHEN, Ralph Alan. "The Function of Setting in *Eastward Ho.*"
*RenP* (1973), 85-96. [London or nearby on the Thames are the only
settings for the play (eighty-three topographical allusions in all).
Place has functions relative to structure and theme: milieus are
solely middle-class, and going "eastward" connotes presumptuous
social ambition.]

---

**Notes and Additions**

**65** LEGGATT, Alexander. *Citizen Comedy in the Age of Shakespeare.* Toronto: Univ. of Toronto Press, 1973. Pp. 47-53. [What some earlier critics accepted as a straightforward Prodigal play is shown to be a most elaborate parody of the genre; its many conventions— trial, imprisonment, repentance, etc.—are *all* there, and much theatrical parody besides.]

## The Gentleman Usher (ca. 1602-1604)

**66** *WEIDNER, Henry M. "The Dramatic Uses of Homeric Idealism: The Significance of Theme and Design in George Chapman's *The Gentleman Usher.*" ELH,* 28 (1961), 121-36. [Basic structure involves contrasted "ceremonies and counter-ceremonies": early, inefficacious masque/game rituals are opposed by later rituals which are beneficial, miraculous, or purificatory.]

**67** MacLURE, Millar. *George Chapman: A Critical Study.* Toronto: Univ. of Toronto Press, 1966. Pp. 95-98. [Noblesse, that quality of gentle mind which is evidenced in virtuous and gracious behavior, thematically differentiates the major characters: those who possess it truly, those who invert or falsely ape it, and Medice, who is utterly deficient in it.]

**68** *SMITH, John Hazel, ed. *The Gentleman Usher.* RRDS. Lincoln: Univ. of Nebraska Press, 1970. Pp. xvi-xxxiii. [Chapman uses satiric, realistic, heroic, and romantic materials from two or three sources and from various comic traditions. Yet, all is unified in respect of theme (the idea of degree) and structure (contrasts/parallels of philosophic attitudes).]

**69** *COPE, Jackson I. *The Theater and the Dream: From Metaphor to Form in Renaissance Drama.* Baltimore: Johns Hopkins Univ. Press, 1973. Pp. 33-52. [Theme and structure are fully and convincingly analyzed in light of Chapman's familiarity with Ficinian Neoplatonism and the myth of Hercules, as apotheosized in the mythographies of Cartari and Ripa.]

---

*Monsieur D'Olive* (1605)

**70**    *HOGAN, A.P. "Thematic Unity in Chapman's *Monsieur D'Olive.*"
         *SEL,* 11 (1971), 295-306. [Thematic unity and the structural
         interconnections of plot and subplot are keyed to the Neoplatonic
         idea that ultimate reality is a transcendental form rather than its
         finite, corporeal embodements. Imagery (e.g., gestation-birth-
         rebirth) conveys a cyclic form.]

*The Revenge of Bussy D'Ambois* (ca. 1601-1612)

**71**    AGGELER, Geoffrey. "The Unity of Chapman's *The Revenge of
         Bussy D'Ambois.*" *PCP,* 4 (1969), 5-18. [Epictetus's *Discourses,*
         specifically in its two mythical exemplars of heroic *virtù,* Hercules
         and Odysseus, gave Chapman a totally different Stoic model for
         Clermont, in whom wrongful, private revenge must be reconciled
         with a public, moral purpose.]

**72**    *BERGSON, Allen. "The Worldly Stoicism of George Chapman's
         *The Revenge of Bussy D'Ambois* and *The Tragedy of Chabot,
         Admiral of France.*" *PQ,* 55 (1976), 43-64. [Clermont's Stoic
         otherworldliness and rationalistic bias are ironically undercut by
         his failure to see a palpable ghost, and by the physical, world-
         centered idiom of his antesuicide speeches.]

**73**    DEMERS, Patricia. "Chapman's *The Revenge of Bussy D'Ambois:*
         Fixity and the Absolute Man." *Ren&R,* 12 (1976), 12-20.
         [Clermont's fixity consists in his lifelong, Epictetan devotion to
         learning, which both crowns the man and affords the play's
         vitalizing ideal; fire, blood, and marine images also distinguish
         him ehtically from the less favored characters.]

*The Tragedy of Chabot, Admiral of France* (rev. by J. Shirley; 1611-
         1622?)

**74**    *RIBNER, Irving. *Jacobean Tragedy: The Quest for Moral Order.*
         New York: Barnes & Noble, 1962. Pp. 35-49. [One's reading of this

pessimistic view, with its stress upon human frailty and imperfection, and failed idealism, ought to take into account objections raised by Thelma Herring, "Chapman and an Aspect of Modern Criticism," *RenD*, 8 (1965), 167-79.]

75    STAGG, Louis Charles. "Characterization Through Nature Imagery in the Tragedies of George Chapman." *BSUF*, 9 (1968), 39-43. [Nature imagery supplies correlates of the heroic protagonist himself: as a magnificent star, a mighty sun in eclipse, a dying tree, as one subjected to figurative whirlwinds, lightning, and buffeting from "impetuous waves."]

76    BRAUNMULLER, A.R. " 'A Greater Wound': Corruption and Human Frailty in Chapman's *Chabot, Admiral of France*." *MLR*, 70 (1975), 241-59. [A milieu of corruption, despair, immorality, injustice, and hatred and envy of goodness surrounds the central, personal conflict between the saintly, proud hero and his king. The tragedy excels as a play of ideas.]

77    BERGSON, Allen. "The Worldly Stoicism of George Chapman's *The Revenge of Bussy D'Ambois* and *The Tragedy of Chabot, Admiral of France*." *PQ*, 55 (1976), 43-64. [Chabot is heroic in his devotion to justice as a Stoic absolute; but ironic too, for his anger, stubbornness, and political naivete augur a tragic facing (see the violence imagery) with reality.]

*The Widow's Tears* (1603-1609)

78    SCHOENBAUM, Samuel. "*The Widow's Tears* and the Other Chapman." *HLQ*, 23 (1960), 321-38. [Though the play's misogyny and cynicism are questionably grounded on the biographical fallacy ("[Tharsalio] is the dramatist's spokesman, and his vision is also Chapman's"), the essay does treat the thematic motifs of honor, Tharsalio's "poison" and "confidence."]

79    *WEIDNER, Henry M. "Homer and the Fallen World: Focus of Satire in George Chapman's *The Widow's Tears*." *JEGP*, 62 (1963),

518-32. [As satire Chapman presents a radical inversion of the ideal, virtuous world of Homer: Tharsalio (modern corruption's earnest disciple) and Eudora are the fallen Ulysses and Penelope in ironic parallels to the *Odyssey*.]

80   HERRING, Thelma. "Chapman and an Aspect of Modern Criticism." *RenD,* 8 (1965), 153-79. [Tharsalio is often likened to the intriguing slave of New Comedy who controls the action; but a comparison with Old Comedy is also fruitful: Tharsalio is the *eiron* (Ironical type) who exposes the *alazons* (pretentious Impostors), Eudora, Cynthia, and Lysander.]

81   *COPE, Jackson I. *The Theater and the Dream: From Metaphor to Form in Renaissance Drama.* Baltimore: Johns Hopkins Univ. Press, 1973. Pp. 55-75. [The many ironic metamorphoses of human nature in the play are attended to in this excellent close reading of theme and structure; it is especially sensitive to Chapman's means of symbolic expression.]

82   *TRICOMI, Albert H. "The Social Disorder of Chapman's *The Widow's Tears.*" *JEGP,* 72 (1973), 350-59. [Contends Tharsalio to be neither Chapman's spokesman nor a hero; rather, he is an anti-hero, a smug impostor whose triumph over fools like Eudora, the Governor, Cynthia and Lysander represents idealism's negation, the victory of upside-down values.]

# Samuel Daniel

*The Tragedy of Cleopatra* (1593, rev. in 1607)

83   WILLIAMSON, Marilyn L. *Infinite Variety: Antony and Cleopatra in Renaissance Drama and Earlier Tradition.* Mystic, CT: Lawrence Verry, 1974. Pp. 134-49. [Unity is achieved by Cleopatra's heroic stance in contrast to everyone about her, by the choric songs that punctuate each act and counterpoint the action, and by the thematic motif, children.]

**Notes and Additions**

# William Davenant

## *The Platonic Lovers* (1635)

84 *SQUIER, Charles. "Davenant's Comic Assault on *Préciosité: The Platonic Lovers.*" *Univ. of Colorado Studies.* Ed. J.K. Emery. Ser. in Lang. and Lit., 10. Boulder: Univ. of Colorado Press, 1966. Pp. 57-72. [What at times seems a defense of the Platonic love cult is really a devastating satire of it, as analysis of character and structural patterns shows.]

# Thomas Dekker

## *1 The Honest Whore* (with T. Middleton; 1604)

85 URE, Peter. "Patient Madman and Honest Whore: The Middleton-Dekker Oxymoron." *E&S,* 19 (1966), 18-40. [Candido, the "patient madman" of the subplot, like Bellafront of the play's oxymoronic title, is an ironic contradiction; his patience is a *virtue* (not simply a humour) able to convert others. "Transformation" re-echoes in all three plots.]

86 *KISTNER, A.L. and M.K. "*1 Honest Whore:* A Comedy of Blood." *HAB,* 23 (1972), 23-27. ["Blood" occurs thirty-four times, variously denoting family kinship, lust, anger, bloodshed, and guilt; thematically and structurally, the two-fold segments of the plot (the Duke's, Bellafront's) and of the subplot (Candido's, Fustigo's) are unified therein.]

87 *SPIVACK, Charlotte. "Bedlam and Bridewell: Ironic Design in *The Honest Whore.*" *Komos,* 3 (1973), 10-16. [Madness dominates Part I as a thematic web of language (over twenty references), action (symbolic "disguisings" as insane persons), and locale (Bedlam). Paradox, irony, and ambiguity control the vision of life in both parts of the play.]

---

Notes and Additions

## 2 *The Honest Whore* (1604-ca. 1605)

**88**     *MANHEIM, Michael. "The Thematic Structure of Dekker's *2 Honest Whore.*" *SEL*, 5 (1965), 365-81. [The thematic concern of the play, which is to distinguish apparent from real virtue, emerges from its form: a pattern of three, juxtaposed testing situations for Bellafront (II.i, III.ii, IV.i), Matheo (II.i, IV.i, IV.iii), and Hippolito (III.i, IV.i).]

**89**     CHAMPION, Larry S. "From Melodrama to Comedy: A Study of Dramatic Perspective in Dekker's *The Honest Whore,* Parts I and II." *SP,* 69 (1972), 192-209. [Excessively preoccupied with the mechanics and esthetics (viz., "comic tone" or "perspective") of structure rather than with its interpretive uses, the essay does regard the disguises as moral therapy.]

**90**     *SPIVACK, Charlotte. "Bedlam and Bridewell: Ironic Design in *The Honest Whore.*" *Komos,* 3 (1973), 10-16. [Whereas Part I is dominated by the idea of madness, Part II, the bitterer of the two, is characterized by pervasive corruption; images of bestiality (animals, fish, birds, etc.), clothing symbolism, and the Bridewell locale qualify the "happy" ending.]

## *Old Fortunatus* (1599)

**91**     HOMAN, Sidney R., Jr. "*Doctor Faustus,* Dekker's *Old Fortunatus,* and the Morality Plays." *MLQ,* 26 (1965), 497-505. [Homan's arguments—that Dekker's play consciously imitates Marlowe's and that ties are many and strong between *Old Fortunatus* and the morality plays (allegorical characters, etc.)—have been made by others, but with less specificity.]

**92**     *CONOVER, James H. *Thomas Dekker: An Analysis of Dramatic Structure.* SEngL, 38. The Hague: Mouton, 1969. Pp. 51-81. [Mainly concerned with pure dramaturgy, this essay's final section ("Unifying Devices") makes most of its interpretive points, examining repetitive patterns of symbolic actions and images of eating, deformity, disguise, and transformation.]

## *Patient Grissil* (with H. Chettle & W. Haughton; 1600)

93     LEVIN, Richard. *The Multiple Plot in English Renaissance
       Drama*. Chicago: Univ. of Chicago Press, 1971. Pp. 49-51. [Defines
       the relationship of the plot to the subplot as one of direct (but not
       compatible) contrasts—Grissil's "patience" is opposed to
       Gwenthyan's shrewishness, and Gwalter's domestic tyranny
       contrasts with Sir Owen's docility.]

94     KEYISHIAN, Harry. "Griselda on the Elizabethan Stage: The
       *Patient Grissil* of Chettle, Dekker, and Haughton." *SEL*, 16 (1976),
       254-61. [Grissil's accepting her husband's cruel tests seems
       pathological to a modern audience, but choral commentary and the
       subplots reply to our objections. Psychologically, perhaps the story
       rationalizes parental force.]

## *The Roaring Girl* (with T. Middleton; 1611)

95     GOMME, Andor, ed. *The Roaring Girl*. New Mermaids. London:
       Benn, 1976. Pp. xix-xxxii. [An intrigue comedy much like *A Trick*
       and *Michaelmas Term*, but lacking their ironic amorality, this
       sunny play sees virtue victorious. Role-playing, disguises, and
       deceptions (to which the many sexual puns and innuendoes are
       ancillary) contrast appearance and reality.]

## *The Shoemakers' Holiday* (1599)

96     *TOLIVER, Harold E. *"The Shoemakers' Holiday:* Theme and
       Image." *BUSE*, 5 (1961), 208-18. [Human faults are enduring but
       remediable with "the right kind of discipline and the right kind of
       holiday freedom" (p. 208): thematically, dialectical balances are
       struck between true and false honor, love and life's real needs,
       sensual feasting and festivity.]

97     BURELBACH, Frederick M., Jr. "War and Peace in *The*

*Shoemakers' Holiday." TSL,* 13 (1968), 99-107. [Warfare with France is a recurrent reference of the play; although functional (for plot exigencies, evoking patriotism, etc.) it is mainly thematic: war epitomizes other social hostilities which love (in three forms) can transform into peace.]

98      KAPLAN, Joel H. "Virtue's Holiday: Thomas Dekker and Simon Eyre." *RenD,* N.S. 2 (1969), 103-22. [Simon Eyre, embodying sportive madness and commercial opportunism in equal measure, extends the influence of saturnalian mirth and festivity throughout the comedy: three feasts, mentioned or presented, mark the shift of hegemony from local to national realms.]

99      *MANHEIM, Michael. "The Construction of *The Shoemakers' Holiday." SEL,* 10 (1970), 315-23. [Opposite sets of attitudes— duplicity, rigidity vs. integrity, spontaneity—provide a continuous antiphonal pattern until the denouement, when the folk-heroic Henry V arrives as the embodied reconciliation of courtly honor and middle-class pragmatism.]

100     *KINNEY, Arthur F. "Thomas Dekker's *Twelfth Night." UTQ,* 41 (1971), 63-73. [Like the festive revels at court, the play employs saturnalia to effect communal clarification and renewal. Significant are the many allusions to seasonal holidays, the use of mumming disguises, a ritually patterned structure, and Simon Eyre functioning as a Lord of Misrule.]

101     *MORTENSON, Peter. "The Economics of Joy in *The Shoemakers' Holiday." SEL,* 16 (1976), 241-52. [Offsetting the play's cheerful festive comedy and latent pattern of pastoral romance is the idea dominant in all three plots ("one man's gain is another man's loss"), one which reflects the predatory, opportunistic ethos of contemporary mercantilism.]

*The Witch of Edmonton* (with J. Ford & W. Rowley; 1621)

102     WEST, Edward Sackville. "The Significance of *The Witch of*

*Edmonton." Criterion,* 17 (1937), 23-32. [West, while desiring a fuller integration of the play's two actions, those of Frank Thorney and the witch Mother Sawyer, effectually points up their analogous relationship: self-destructiveness (death on the same scaffold) and the conflict of good and evil.]

## John Ford

### *The Broken Heart* (ca. 1625-1633)

103    *BLAYNEY, Glenn H. "Convention, Plot, and Structure in *The Broken Heart." MP,* 56 (1958), 1-9. [Structure is a functional expression of theme: the tragic consequences of an enforced marriage, one the worse for being in violation of a legally binding betrothal, are contrasted with a happy marriage based upon free choice, love, and family consent.]

104    *McDONALD, Charles Osborne. *The Rhetoric of Tragedy: Form in Stuart Drama.* Amherst: Univ. of Massachusetts Press, 1966. Pp. 314-33. [Two iterative verbal antilogies point up central issues: *reason* leads to *knowledge,* producing virtuous *honor;* in opposition stands yet another triad of key words: *passion* leads to *opinion,* producing self-indulgent *content.*]

105    *ANDERSON, Donald K., Jr., ed. *The Broken Heart.* RRDS. Lincoln: Univ. of Nebraska Press, 1968. Pp. xi-xix. [Ford's stylistic hallmarks are as importantly visual, in the form of echoic gestures and postures, as verbal in thematic metaphors. They help to link and contrast the play's characters and to evoke an aesthetic cachet of mannerly decorousness.]

106    *KAUFMANN, R.J. "Ford's 'Waste Land': *The Broken Heart." RenD,* N.S. 3 (1970), 167-88. [This strong essay draws on a full range of modern cirtical resources—myth, depth psychology, mythological (Phaeton especially) and ritual pertinencies, imagery analysis (truncation, blighted growth)—to analogize Sparta with T.S. Eliot's ego-sick "Waste Land."]

107   KELLY, Michael J. "The Values of Action and Chronicle in *The Broken Heart." PLL,* 7 (1971), 150-58. [In a world where man's will is severely limited, where guidance is provided by riddling oracles, characters emphasize transcendence by noble, individual actions (deeds emulatable by posterity) which deserve a chronicle (history's high regard).]

108   *GREENFIELD, Thelma N. "The Language of Process in Ford's *The Broken Heart." PMLA,* 87 (1972), 397-405. [In this play, where Ithocles' initial error "brings inescapable repercussions...on everything that happens" (p. 404), Ford makes heavy use of verbs and verbals, among other techniques, to delineate process—cause and effect in feelings and actions.]

109   *WAITH, Eugene M. "Struggle for Calm: The Dramatic Structure of *The Broken Heart." English Renaissance Drama: Essays in Honor of Madeleine Doran & Mark Eccles.* Ed. S. Henning et al. Carbondale: Southern Illinois Univ. Press, 1976. Pp. 155-66. [Like the psychological theory of musical emotive-cognitive content (expectation temporarily or fully blocked), the play's meaning lies in its pattern of violence avoided.]

*The Fancies, Chaste and Noble* (1635-1636)

110   SUTTON, Juliet. "Platonic Love in Ford's *The Fancies, Chaste and Noble." SEL,* 7 (1967), 299-309. [Central themes are scandal, particularly as regards its power "to transform the truth into its own likeness" (p. 301), distrust, and misinterpretation; *honi soit qui mal y pense* applies to Ford's audience as well as to his dramatic characters.]

*The Lady's Trial* (1638)

111   *HOWE, James. "Ford's *The Lady's Trial:* A Play of Metaphysical Wit." *Genre,* 7 (1974), 342-61. [Legal language is not only thematically crucial in all three plots, emphasizing the analogy between judicial and real-life affairs, but it is also structurally

pertinent, in that all major scenes in the two chief plots are
patterned into clear legal stages.]

## The Lover's Melancholy (1628)

**112**    *STAVIG, Mark. *John Ford and the Traditional Moral Order.*
Madison: Univ. of Wisconsin Press, 1968. Pp. 68-81. [Distinctions
between honest, natural love that is fulfilled in marriage, and
unnatural, lust-inclined "heroical love" (love melancholy), ones
also echoed in an art-nature debate, reflect the Christian, ethical
psychology of Burton's *Anatomy.*]

## Love's Sacrifice (1632?)

**113**    URE, Peter. "Cult and Initiates in Ford's *Love's Sacrifice.*" *MLQ*,
11 (1950), 298-306. [Opposes George F. Sensabaugh's view of Ford
as the proto-modernist exponent of Burtonian determinism
("unbridled individualism"); the play is consistently ethical:
Bianca is the would-be sensualist, Fernando the upholder of male
friendship and Platonic love.]

**114**    *STAVIG, Mark. *John Ford and the Traditional Moral Order.*
Madison: Univ. of Wisconsin Press, 1968. Pp. 122-43. [Platonic
theories of love, by which physical passion and beauty are so
glorified that libertinism and tragedy are consequences, affect
almost every character in the play. Structure and stagecraft help to
assert Ford's moral point of view.]

**115**    McMASTER, Juliet. "Love, Lust, and Sham: Structural Pattern in
the Plays of John Ford." *RenD*, N.S. 2 (1969), 157-66. [*Love's
Sacrifice* provides a clear example of Ford's usual triple-plot
pattern, in which typically kinds of sexual relationships are
contrasted: true love, with restrained desire; lust, with multiple
liaisons; and satiric sham love.]

## Perkin Warbeck (ca. 1625-1634)

**116** ANDERSON, Donald K., Jr. "Kingship in Ford's *Perkin Warbeck.*" *ELH,* 27 (1960), 177-93. [Deviation from his sources in Bacon and Gainsford confirms Ford's structural scheme of portraying alternate versions of kingship in James, Warbeck, and Henry, the latter being the practical ideal for wisdom, foresight, economy, use of counsel, and promotion of peace.]

**117** *WEATHERS, Winston. *"Perkin Warbeck:* A Seventeenth-Century Psychological Play." *SEL,* 4 (1964), 217-26. [A most original, perhaps brilliant, psychological-mythopoeic interpretation: Kings Henry and James symbolize cold rationality and passion, antitheses whose balance in one psychic "self" is upset by a neurosis (the mad Warbeck) which must be purged.]

**118** URE, Peter, ed. *The Chronicle History of Perkin Warbeck: A Strange Truth.* Revels Plays. London: Methuen, 1968. Pp. xlv-lxxxiii. [Ure's essay is more a polished, scene-by-scene résumé of style and technique than an analysis; nevertheless, comments upon character (a premium on "civility"), structure, and stagecraft point up altering perspectives.]

**119** BARISH, Jonas A. *"Perkin Warbeck* as Anti-History." *EIC,* 20 (1970), 151-71. [Critics (except T.S. Eliot) wrongly assume that Ford's view *must* be that of de facto history and his sources, the historians who ratified Henry VII's legitimacy and vilified Perkin as an impostor; but Ford is shown to have suspended judgment, for no evidence is conclusive.]

**120** *COPE, Jackson I. *The Theater and the Dream: From Metaphor to Form in Renaissance Drama.* Baltimore: Johns Hopkins Univ. Press, 1973. Pp. 122-33. [Finds the pretended-prince *scenari* of *commedia dell'arte* a derived influence upon the play, whose thematic concern with acting and actuality, shadow and substance involves epistemological perspectivism.]

**121** *NEILL, Michael. " 'Anticke Pageantrie': The Mannerist Art of *Perkin Warbeck.*" *RenD,* N.S. 7 (1976), 117-50. [Ford's play is a

bravura piece of self-referential mannerist art, paralleling
Warbeck's *maniera* constancy in his assumed role. "Honor"
(absent from Henry's pragmatic kingship) and "truth," like the
conscious histrionism, betoken paradoxical values.]

## *'Tis Pity She's a Whore* (1629?-1633)

**122**   ANDERSON, Donald K., Jr. "The Heart and the Banquet:
Imagery in Ford's *'Tis Pity* and *The Broken Heart.*" *SEL,* 2 (1962),
209-17. [Giovanni's climactic appearance at Soranzo's feast with
the torn-out heart of Annabella makes tragically literal what heart,
banquet, food, and feast imageries figured earlier through ironic
associations with physical love.]

**123**   RIBNER, Irving. *Jacobean Tragedy: The Quest for Moral Order.*
New York: Barnes & Noble, 1962. Pp. 163-74. [Ford's paradoxy
reflects Caroline scepticism: man faces the dilemma of having to
conform to inadequate religious mores and flawed social codes
(depicted in the interrelated subplots), or living solely by nature's
light, which can only lead to error.]

**124**   BAWCUTT, N.W., ed. *'Tis Pity She's a Whore.* RRDS. Lincoln:
Univ. of Nebraska Press, 1966. Pp. xi-xxii. [This sensible
introduction accommodates the divergent ethical responses to the
play, particularly as they relate to the thematic motifs of fate,
heaven (used more than thirty times), and justice, and to the three
leading characters as well.]

**125**   MORRIS, Brian, ed. *'Tis Pity She's a Whore.* New Mermaids.
London: Benn, 1968. Pp. viii-xxvi. [Ford remains coolly objective
towards his subject, accepting the repugnance of incest but placing
stress on the social perspective: isolation of the lovers in relation to
their corrupt environment. Emblematic spectacle and key
metaphors help convey meaning.]

**126**   *STAVIG, Mark. *John Ford and the Traditional Moral Order.*
Madison: Univ. of Wisconsin Press, 1968. Pp. 95-121. [An orthodox

Christian moral framework is said to obtain: Giovanni, talented and virtuous at first, succumbs to heroical love, twists contemporary Platonic love theorems (a satirical thrust), progressively degrading himself and Annabella.]

127    *ROSEN, CAROL C. "The Language of Cruelty in Ford's *'Tis Pity She's a Whore."* *CompD,* 8 (1974), 356-68. [Antonin Artaud's use of Ford's play as a paradigm for the Theater of Cruelty is the basis of a detailed reading of its savage, primordial modes of expressing cruelty—verbally (plague, decay) and theatrically (abusive tone, ritualized actions).]

128    CHAMPION, Larry S. "Ford's *'Tis Pity She's a Whore* and the Jacobean Tragic Perspective." *PMLA,* 90 (1975), 78-87. [Not a study that breaks new ground, but valuable nonetheless for its full appreciation of how nearly every surrounding character places the protagonists in a decadent social context, distancing their sin; thus, moral ambivalence is pervasive.]

# Robert Greene

*Friar Bacon and Friar Bungay* (ca. 1589-1592)

129    EMPSON, William. *Some Versions of Pastoral.* London: Chatto & Windus, 1935. Pp. 31-34. [A pioneer evaluation of how apparently diverse segments of Greene's double plot form a unity in juxtaposition: it is because Margaret's beauty and Bacon's magic are metaphorically similar powers, both being "individualist, dangerous, and outside the social order."]

130    *ASSARSSON-RIZZI, Kerstin. *"Friar Bacon and Friar Bungay":* *A Structural and Thematic Analysis of Robert Greene's Play.* LSE, 44. Lund: C.W.K. Gleerup, 1972. [Not all insights into form and style in this 154-page study have interpretive value (or make for stimulating reading), but many do—among them are notions of illusion, love, and the social order, etc.]

Notes and Additions

131    *MORTENSON, Peter. *"Friar Bacon and Friar Bungay:* Festive
        Comedy and 'Three-Form'd Luna.' " *ELR,* 2 (1972), 194-207.
        ["Misrule," in the form of Edward's lust and Bacon's black magic,
        designates the first of the play's two movements as a festive
        comedy; "pageant" culminates in sc. xvi, when historical-
        mythographic symbolism underpins mythopoeic ritual.]

132    SENN, Werner. "Robert Greene's Handling of Source Material in
        *Friar Bacon and Friar Bungay." ES,* 54 (1973), 544-53. [More
        interpretive than the author's formalistic approach in *Studies in
        the Dramatic Construction of Robert Greene and George Peele*
        (Bern, 1973), this essay treats numerous interplot analogies,
        parallels, and contrasts which are thematic.]

133    *WERTHEIM, Albert. "The Presentation of Sin in *Friar Bacon and
        Friar Bungay." Criticism,* 16 (1974), 273-86. [Bacon's necromantic
        powers, displayed in a series of episodes, emerge as increasingly
        destructive; in the process, the Seven Deadly Sins are revealed in
        Bacon himself and others. Didactically, Margaret's virtues offset
        these sins in her plot.]

134    *WELD, John. *Meaning in Comedy: Studies in Elizabethan
        Romantic Comedy.* Albany: State Univ. of New York Press, 1975.
        Pp. 136-53. [Noting that each of the main plots builds to a climactic
        repentance scene that leads its protagonist to a joyful ending, Weld
        analyzes the several plots, paying close attention to theatrical
        details which are visual symbols.]

## *A Looking Glass for London and England* (with T. Lodge; 1587-1591)

135    PASACHOFF, Naomi E. *Playwrights, Preachers, and Politicians:
        A Study of Four Tudor Old Testament Dramas.* ElizS, 45. Salzburg,
        Aust.: Univ. of Salzburg, 1975. Pp. 57-98. [Tudor sermons relate
        symbiotically to the play, but not as direct sources: four corrupt
        social estates (priests and the prophet Jonah being one) comprise
        four intertwining plots.]

---

**Notes and Additions**

*Orlando Furioso* (with S. Rowley?; 1588-1592)

**136**    GELBER, Norman. "Robert Greene's *Orlando Furioso:* A Study of
Thematic Ambiguity." *MLR,* 64 (1969), 264-66. [Apparent
ambiguity surrounds a major thematic idea, misogyny, as it relates
in particular to the heroine, Angelica. It is resolved by seeing the
three potent antifeminine speeches in context, as a moral foil for
that female paragon of virtue.]

**137**    BABULA, William. "Fortune or Fate: Ambiguity in Robert
Greene's *Orlando Furioso.*" *MLR,* 67 (1972), 481-85. [Incompatible
views as to destiny's controlling force do create a thematic polarity:
providence (purposeful, moral justice) or fortune (chaotic, amoral
chance); but, one might wish more proof that Greene leaves the
matter unresolved, ambiguous.]

*The Scottish History of James IV* (ca. 1590-1591)

**138**    *SANDERS, Norman, ed. *The Scottish History of James the Fourth.*
Revels Plays. London: Methuen, 1970. Pp. xxxvi-lv. [Agrees with
critics who find morality-play figures behind the King, Ateukin,
and others, but emphasizes Dorothea's being the Patient Griselda
archetype. Bohan and Oberon bridge the audience-actor barrier,
which has critical implications.]

**139**    BRAUNMULLER, A.R. "The Serious Comedy of Greene's *James
IV.*" *ELR,* 3 (1973), 335-50. [Greene exaggerates the literary,
unnatural quality of the interior romance play; complicated
theatrical illusion and inverted coventions are means by which the
pat romantic solutions are distanced, and thus qualified. For this
reason, the play is more complex.]

## Thomas Heywood

*The English Traveller* (1621-1633)

**140**    *GRIVELET, Michel. "The Simplicity of Thomas Heywood." *ShS,*

14 (1961), 56-65. [Heywood's alleged simplicity is exploded in this deceptively titled essay centering on thematic and structural unity in this one play. A complex interplay of characters' functions and symbolic names, and such symbolic ideas as *travel* and *house,* weave plot and subplot together.]

141   *RABKIN, Norman. "Dramatic Deception in Heywood's *The English Traveller.*" *SEL,* 1 (1961), 1-16. [Appearance and reality is the "supreme analogue" of structure (plot and subplot involve a dissembler's unmasking), character (January-May lovers, the moral courtesan, and the witty servant alternately answer to and invert conventions), and imagery.]

## 1 The Fair Maid of the West (1609-1610)

142   *SALOMON, Brownell, ed. *Thomas Heywood's "The Fair Maid of the West," Part I: A Critical Edition.* With an Introd. and Notes. JDS, 36. Salzburg, Aust.: Univ. of Salzburg, 1975. Pp. 36-58. [Central character and structure both involve a balanced fusion of the realistic and romantic modes. Supplies a full thematic reading and a structuralist analysis of the underlying archetype, the adventure-quest myth.]

## Love's Mistress (1634)

143   *COPE, Jackson I. *The Theater and the Dream: From Metaphor to Form in Renaissance Drama.* Baltimore: Johns Hopkins Univ. Press, 1973. Pp. 173-96. [Argues that the play is not primarily about Psyche, but about Apuleius who, as "author"-participant, enacts with Psyche his personal resurrection ritual. Cope's style is rarely so diffuse as here.]

## The Rape of Lucrece (1606-1608)

144   *RIBNER, Irving. *Jacobean Tragedy: The Quest for Moral Order.* New York: Barnes & Noble, 1962. Pp. 58-71. [Strongly influenced by Shakespeare's *Macbeth,* the play concerns the interdependence

of private, public, and cosmic evil. As the first of its two movements, Rome's all-pervasive corruption is shown, followed by a providential restitution of order.]

## A Woman Killed with Kindness (1603)

145     *SPACKS, Patricia Meyer. "Honor and Perception in *A Woman Killed with Kindness.*" *MLQ,* 20 (1959), 321-32. [Five main characters (Frankford's wife, Wendoll, Acton, Mountford, and Susan) demonstrate in varying ways failures of honor; Frankford's lack of perception negates his honor; only Nick is honorable and perceptive in a world of false appearances.]

146     VAN FOSSEN, R.W., ed. *A Woman Killed with Kindness.* Revels Plays. Cambridge, MA: Harvard Univ. Press, 1961. Pp. xxvii-lviii. [Van Fossen's is the standard edition, and the introduction assembles several kernels of value from earlier criticism. But indeed, theme, structure, characters, and style are reviewed topically, not as interrelated aspects.]

147     COOK, David. *"A Woman Killed with Kindness:* An Unshakespearian Tragedy." *ES,* 45 (1964), 353-72. [Once the play's producer at the University of London, Cook gives detailed impressions of Heywood's simple, direct, yet intense characterizations of Frankford, Anne, and Wendoll, though attention is also paid to the relatedness of plot and subplot.]

148     *CANUTESON, John. "The Theme of Forgiveness in the Plot and Subplot of *A Woman Killed with Kindness.*" *RenD,* N.S. 2 (1969), 123-41. [Sees Frankford as no paragon of Christian forgiveness whose self-realization comes at last; his judgment remains revengeful despite pretensions to charity. Analogically, Mountford reduces honor to the absurd.]

149     LEVIN, Richard. *The Multiple Plot in English Renaissance Drama.* Chicago: Univ. of Chicago Press, 1971. Pp. 93-97. [Structure is a variant of the three-level hierarchical formula; plot

Notes and Additions

levels reflect differentiated classes (knightly, bourgeois, servants'),
but Frankford's takes precedence, inverting social priority for
ethical and esthetic purposes.]

150    *BRYAN, Margaret B. "Food symbolism in *A Woman Killed with
       Kindness." RenP* (1974), 9-17. ["Heywood consistently uses eating
       to represent erotic love or lust, specifically that of Wendoll for
       Anne" (p. 9)—allowing us a Freudian view of Frankford's neurosis.
       Reinforcing verbal references to food in the play is the structural
       pattern of three meals.]

151    *RAUCHBAUER, Otto. "Visual and Rhetorical Imagery in Th.
       Heywood's *A Woman Killed with Kindness." ES,* 57 (1976), 200-10.
       [Using a semiological approach, whereby verbal and nonverbal
       theatrical elements are all viewed as contributing to meaning,
       Rauchbauer treats the didactic purpose of metaphors (music; the
       dance) and of emblematic motifs and tableaux.]

## Thomas Hughes

*The Misfortunes of Arthur* (with F. Bacon, N. Trotte, W. Fulbeck, J.
Lancaster, C. Yelverton, W. Penroodock, & F. Flower; 1588)

152    ARMSTRONG, William A. "Elizabethan Themes in *The
       Misfortunes of Arhtur." RES,* 7 (1956), 238-49. [Seneca's influence
       is undeniable—but not overwhelming—in the stress upon a tainted
       royal family and in the rhetoric. Ideas and images of usurpation,
       political ambition, and civil rebellion give it an ethos more like that
       of the Elizabethan chronicle play.]

## Ben Jonson

*The Alchemist* (1610)

153    GOODMAN, Paul. *The Structure of Literature.* Chicago: Univ. of

Chicago Press, 1954. Pp. 80-100. [*The Alchemist* is the most fully worked out Jonsonian comic action of "pure deflation," and, viewed as an exemplary comedy of intrigue, is well served by this neo-Aristotelian "inductive formal analysis." Character types are assigned a taxonomy by function.]

154 *PARTRIDGE, Edward B. *The Broken Compass: A Study of the Major Comedies of Ben Jonson.* New York: Columbia Univ. Press, 1958. Pp. 114-60. [Imagery is functional: comic indecorum results from base *tenors'* being related to great *vehicles* (gold/god, Dol/Queen, etc.) by means of inflated epithets, and by religious, alchemical, and commercial terminology.]

155 *THAYER, C.G. *Ben Jonson: Studies in the Plays.* Norman: Univ. of Oklahoma Press, 1963. Pp. 84-111. [Alchemy is simultaneously a confidence game and, through the crucial alchemical dialogue (II.iii.133-98) functioning as an Aristophanic *agon,* a metaphor for comic art. Symbolic structure reinforces theme, for Subtle's "art" metamorphoses society.]

156 BLISSETT, William. "The Venter Tripartite in *The Alchemist.*" *SEL,* 8 (1968), 323-34. [Analysis of their names, appearance, and traits shows that Face, Dol Common, and Subtle are, respectively, analogues of that infamous trio of mankind's enemies in the morality play: the World, the Flesh, and the Devil; Sir Epicure plays Carnal Imagination's role.]

157 HOLLERAN, James V. "Character Transmutation in *The Alchemist.*" *CLAJ,* 11 (1968), 221-27. [More than a duping mechanism, alchemy supplies the method of characterization: gulls and crooks alike would "transmute" themselves to ideal beings; Lovewit restores reality. Progressively, Face's various assumed roles decline in status, but Subtle's augment.]

158 *DESSEN, Alan C. *Jonson's Moral Comedy.* Evanston, IL: Northwestern Univ. Press, 1971. Pp. 105-37. [Finds a basis for the general structure and parts of the action in the late morality play;

in particular, Ananias and Epicure Mammon symbolize two major "estates," the clergy and knighthood, that fail of social obligation in a gold-dominated world.]

159     *DONALDSON, Ian. "Language, Noise, and Nonsense: *The Alchemist.*" *Seventeenth-Century Imagery: Essays on Uses of Figurative Language from Donne to Farquhar.* Ed. E. Miner. Berkeley: Univ. of California Press, 1971. Pp. 69-82. [Language constantly modulates into "parody, rant, and cant, into mock-heroic, foreign, and nonsensical speech, and finally into mere noise" (p. 73); talking promotes social fragmentation, and is a substitute for doing and achieving.]

*Bartholomew Fair* (1614)

160     *BARISH, Jonas A. *Ben Jonson and the Language of Prose Comedy.* Cambridge, MA: Harvard Univ. Press, 1960. Pp. 188-239. [Examines lexical and syntactical aspects of style in detail to define both character, as in the relation of Busy's sham biblicality to Adam's mock Latinity, and theme, which is human physicality, perversity, and littleness.]

161     *ROBINSON, James E. *"Bartholomew Fair:* Comedy of Vapors." *SEL,* 1 (1961), 65-80. [Vapors, described as bilious symptoms of passion or physiological disorder in Renaissance treatises, are made by Jonson the play's central symbolism—in imagery, characterization, and action—of man's animal nature and folly.]

162     *COPE, Jackson I. *"Bartholomew Fair* as Blasphemy." *RenD,* 8 (1965), 127-52. [One may resist Cope's premise, that Jonson here intended a profane anti-morality play which denies divine providence, and yet value the thematic, emblematic, and Scriptural analyses tying idea (commercialism, the blindness of legalism and Old Testament justice) and physical action.]

163     *DONALDSON, Ian. *The World Upside-Down: Comedy from Jonson to Fielding.* Oxford: Clarendon Press, 1970. Pp. 46-77.

[*Licence,* somewhat of a unifying pun in this tonally complex work, is one of many ironic devices by which freedoms and restraints are brought into question and qualified. Resemblances between reality and play-world give a double focus.]

164    *PARKER, R.B. "The Themes and Staging of *Bartholomew Fair.*" *UTQ,* 39 (1970), 293-309. [Studies interpretively important examples of emblematic staging or decor: the three main locales at the fair are "symbolic loci," representing the fair's influence on appetite (the pig booth), law (the stocks), and art (the puppet booth).]

165    *DESSEN, Alan C. *Jonson's Moral Comedy.* Evanston, IL: Northwestern Univ. Press, 1971. Pp. 138-220. [Jonson, it is argued, employs the morality play's structure and techniques to demonstrate that social maladies (represented by the Fair) prevail when *manqués* authority figures in education, religion, and justice fail to exert influence over average humanity.]

166    *LEVIN, Richard. *The Multiple Plot in English Renaissance Drama.* Chicago: Univ. of Chicago Press, 1971. Pp. 202-14. [A classic essay which proves how carefully articulated is Jonson's structure, which to some appears plotless. The fair visitors, the "wits," and Overdo form symmetrical, analogous groups which temporally interact, disintegrate and realign.]

## The Case is Altered (1597-1598)

167    *ENCK, John J. *Jonson and the Comic Truth.* Madison: Univ. of Wisconsin Press, 1957. Pp. 21-3. [Self-deception and misjudging by false appearances are the leading concerns: "The plot always turns on an aspect of comprehending personality; the figurative language refers repeatedly to it; from the outset the costumes reinforce it" (pp. 25-26).]

## Catiline His Conspiracy (1611)

---

**Notes and Additions**

168   ENCK, John J. *Jonson and the Comic Truth.* Madison: Univ. of
      Wisconsin Press, 1957. Pp. 172-88. [Reasons for the failure of this
      play are treated at length. Interpretively, the pervasive lethargy is
      noted as being an important thematic effect: frustrated resolve,
      lassitude, and inactivity are recurrent ideas, as is the imagery of
      listless animals.]

169   HILL, Geoffrey. "The World's Proportion: Jonson's Poetry in
      *Sejanus* and *Catiline.*" *Jacobean Theatre.* Ed. J.R. Brown and B.
      Harris. Stratford-upon-Avon Studies, 1. New York: St. Martin's,
      1960. Pp. 113-31. [Of analytical value, in an essay that treats both
      Roman tragedies simultaneously, are comments on the sex-role
      reversals and the ironic epithets.]

170   *JACKSON, Gabriele Bernhard. *Vision and Judgment in Ben
      Jonson's Drama.* New Haven: Yale Univ. Press, 1968. Pp. 128-35 et
      passim. ["*Catiline* is The Play of Masks: those who don them
      reveal themselves" (p. 132). Contrasts between "face" and "visor"
      (essential nobility and deceit), and light and dark are among the
      valuative key words and image patterns.]

171   *BOLTON, W.F., and Jane F. GARDNER, eds. *Catiline.* RRDS.
      Lincoln: Univ. of Nebraska Press, 1973. Pp. xi-xxiv. [With
      remarkable economy, given the exigencies of a brief introduction,
      the authors treat the unifying functions of imagery (sexuality,
      rebellion against the gods, theatricality, etc.) and structural
      scheme (symmetrical first and last scenes.).]

*Cynthia's Revels* (1600)

172   *GILBERT, Allan H. "The Function of the Masques in *Cynthia's
      Revels.*" *PQ*, 22 (1943), 211-30. [The two masques in Act V, in which
      vices disguise themselves as virtues, reflect the comedy's main
      concern: to make the revels a satirical occasion for reforming
      courtly follies like egotism and fatuity, for a monarch has a duty to
      set his subjects a good example.]

173     TALBERT, Ernest William. "The Classical Mythology and the
        Structure of *Cynthia's Revels.*" *PQ,* 22 (1943), 193-210.
        [Mythological elements are essential to the overall design;
        moralizations of the Actaeon, Niobe, Echo, and Narcissus myths,
        which Jonson found in familiar mythographies, aid his urging
        Stoic virtue, not self-love, as the courtly ideal.]

174     THRON, E.M. "Jonson's *Cynthia's Revels:* Multiplicity and
        Unity." *SEL,* 11 (1971), 235-47. [Wölfflin's concept of multiple unity
        (independent parts related through a common idea), formulated to
        describe cinquecentist art, applies to Jonson's undramatic use of
        mythological, satirical, and masque genres. Flattery and self-love
        are major themes.]

## *The Devil Is an Ass* (1616)

175     *THAYER, C.G. *Ben Jonson: Studies in the Plays.* Norman: Univ. of
        Oklahoma Press, 1963. Pp. 156-77. [Pug, a real but harmless devil
        in a subplot parodying the morality play, has an analogue in
        Fitzdottrell, the devilish ass of the main plot. As its Platonic moral
        argument the play opposes the love of material things to the love of
        virtue.]

176     *CHAMPION, Larry S. *Ben Jonson's "Dotages": A Reconsideration
        of the Late Plays.* Lexington: Univ. of Kentucky Press, 1967. Pp. 22-
        44. [Classical five-act structure affords coherence and is
        functional, for the allegorical morality figures appear only in the
        protasis and the catastrophe, thus framing and giving satiric
        perspective to earthly vices.]

177     DESSEN, Alan C. *Jonson's Moral Comedy.* Evanston, IL:
        Northwestern Univ. Press, 1971. Pp. 221-35. [For his own devil
        play, Jonson violates audience expectations by inverting the
        morality play's devil-Vice helpmeet relationship: "modern"
        earthlings like Wittipol and the Vice-figure Meercraft outdo in evil
        Satan's inept emissary, Pug the devil.]

---

Notes and Additions

*Epicoene* (1609)

178    *HEFFNER, Ray L., Jr. "Unifying Symbols in the Comedy of Ben
       Jonson." *English Stage Comedy*. Ed. W.K. Wimsatt, Jr. New York:
       Columbia Univ. Press, 1955. Pp. 74-97. [Dryden's *Essay of
       Dramatic Poesy* to the contrary, the play's unity is not neoclassic
       but thematic: noise is the central symbol, with noisy people
       standing opposed to the noise haters.]

179    *PARTRIDGE, Edward B. *The Broken Compass: A Study of the
       Major Comedies of Ben Jonson*. New York: Columbia Univ. Press,
       1958. Pp. 161-77. [Abnormal sexual ambiguity provides the key
       metaphor for deviations from social and sexual norms of decorum.
       Unnatural role-reversals are pandemic, as "Nearly everyone in the
       play is epicene in some way" (p. 162).]

180    *BARISH, Jonas A. *Ben Jonson and the Language of Prose
       Comedy*. Cambridge, MA: Harvard Univ. Press, 1960. Pp. 142-86.
       [Splendid analyses of each major character's rhetorical uniqueness
       (pp. 149-74) are followed by a psychological approach to theme: life
       values are opposed by those of death, anti-social solitude,
       impotence, frigidity—the epicene.]

181    THAYER, C.G. *Ben Jonson: Studies in the Plays*. Norman: Univ. of
       Oklahoma Press, 1963. Pp. 66-84. [The aberrant, inverted nature of
       society is Jonson's subject, for which the central symbol is an
       impossible ideal—a silent woman. As the dominant symbolic
       expression of folly there is La-Fool's dinner party in Act III, a
       secular *festa stultorum*.]

182    ANDERSON, Mark A. "The Successful Unity of *Epicoene*: A
       Defense of Ben Jonson." *SEL*, 10 (1970), 349-66. [Unity lies in the
       formal coherence of *Epicoene's* plots, in which society's proneness
       to deception is exposed: the subplots "parallel the main actions and
       situations, illuminating Morose and his situation with
       exaggerations and contrasts" (p. 358).]

---

**183** *DONALDSON, Ian. *The World Upside-Down: Comedy from Jonson to Fielding.* Oxford: Clarendon, 1970. Pp. 78-98. [In that the contrast between "secret" and "open" people, between private and public life, is central to *Epicoene,* the punitive attack on Morose's isolation by means of a festive, *charivari*-like ceremony (III.vi-vii) is thus the leading action.]

**184** *SLIGHTS, William W.E. "*Epicoene* and the Prose Paradox." *PQ,* 49 (1970), 178-87. [Paradoxy, with its tortuous logic and equivoca-tions, colors all thought in the play: as rhetorical paradox, in signi-ficant portions of the dialogue; and as logical paradox, which informs the serial ordering of actions and the characters' role-reversals and mixed natures.]

## *Every Man in His Humour* (1598)

**185** BARISH, Jonas A. *Ben Jonson and the Language of Prose Comedy.* Cambridge, MA: Harvard Univ. Press, 1960. Pp. 98-104. [Jonson's prose is confident here; the 1616 Folio revision added much, changed little. Style is a moral index, descriminating each folly: e.g., Bobadilla's cant, his schemata, and "I"-pronoun fixation sketch his self-delusion.]

**186** BRYANT, J.A., Jr. "Jonson's Revision of *Every Man in His Humor.*" *SP,* 59 (1962), 641-50. [While the 1598 version overburdened the New Comedy intrigue in its concerns with humour theory and poetry's social role, the Folio version is a masterful humour play in which characterization integrates with a symptoms-aggravation-crisis-cure structural pattern.]

**187** LEVER, J.W., ed. "*Every Man in His Humour*": A Parallel-Text Edition of the 1601 Quarto and the 1616 Folio.* RRDS. Lincoln: Univ. of Nebraska Press, 1971. Pp. xii-xx. ["Snobbery is the universal folly derided in *Every Man in His Humour,* whose real key word is not 'humour' but 'gentleman' " (p. xvi). Braggarts, gulls, and gallants are all infected.]

188   LEVIN, Lawrence L. "Clement Justice in *Every Man in his Humor.*" *SEL,* 12 (1972), 291-307. [Clement Justice, the most flattering embodiment of law and order in Jonsonian drama, represents juridically the ideal Aristotelian norm; he reinforces a central theme, the proper use of language, and, symbolically, is also priest, educator, and poet.]

189   WILLIAMS, Mary C. *Unity in Ben Jonson's Early Comedies.* JDS, 22. Salzburg, Aust.: Univ. of Salzburg, 1972. Pp. 92-120. [*Every Man In* employs schematic character parallels and contrasts in accordance with a controlling idea, a "humour structure": the exposure and punishment (or reform) of humours. Imagery underscores the strife of passion and reason.]

190   COLLEY, John Scott. "Opinion, Poetry, and Folly in *Every Man in His Humor.*" *SAB,* 39 (1974), 10-21. [Opinion, that malady of self-deception and moral blindness of which men may still be cured by a dose of reason, is the organizing idea and ethical basis of the Quarto version; revised, the play stresses intrigue, not comic-satirical moral emblems.]

## *Every Man out of His Humour* (1599)

191   BARISH, Jonas A. *Ben Jonson and the Language of Prose Comedy.* Cambridge, MA: Harvard Univ. Press, 1960. Pp. 104-13. [Grotesqueries of language and rhetorical innovations that strain plausibility are more elaborate in this play than hitherto. In Fastidious, Sordido, and the rest, specific linguistic vices are welded to their moral equivalents.]

192   *COPE, Jackson I. *The Theater and the Dream: From Metaphor to Form in Renaissance Drama.* Baltimore: Johns Hopkins Univ. Press, 1973. Pp. 226-36. [Dramatic form reflects the paradox of illusion, chiefly through the author-satirist figure (Buffone-Macilente-Asper-"Ben Jonson") by whom the "doubleness of acting and watching" extends to many levels.]

*The Magnetic Lady* (1632)

193    PARTRIDGE, Edward B. *The Broken Compass: A Study of the Major Comedies of Ben Jonson.* New York: Columbia Univ. Press, 1958. Pp. 205-12. [Jonson's emphasis on decorum produces a "strong texture, tight, formalized, and symbolic" (p. 209), but another result is predictable imagery with familiar tenor-vehicle relationships, such as the linking of sex and money.]

194    THAYER, C.G. *Ben Jonson: Studies in the Plays.* Norman: Univ. of Oklahoma Press, 1963. Pp. 232-46. [Sees the characters' roles and their pattern of marriages as a symbolic synthesis: "The comic artist [Compass]...is joined with that which is pleasing and agreeable [Pleasance]. Ironside, morality, marries Lady Lodestone, nature" (p. 244).]

195    CHAMPION, Larry S. *Ben Jonson's "Dotages": A Reconsideration of the Late Plays.* Lexington: Univ. of Kentucky Press, 1967. Pp. 104-30. [The play "is an allegorical declamation of proper comedy with Compass symbolizing the poet-entertainer, Ironside the poet-moralist, Lady Loadstone and her house the theater[, and]...Pleasance the spectator" (p. 116).]

196    McFARLAND, Ronald E. "Jonson's *Magnetic Lady* and the Reception of Gilbert's *De Magnete.*" *SEL,* 11 (1971), 283-93. [Magnetism is not only the governing metaphor of the play, its technical information supplying charactonyms and wordplays, but as a structural principle it controls characters' relationships (e.g., Compasse finds out the true Steele).]

*The New Inn* (1629)

197    *PARTRIDGE, Edward B. *The Broken Compass: A Study of the Major Comedies of Ben Jonson.* New York: Columbia Univ. Press, 1958. Pp. 189-205. [Characters' violations of decorum by word and deed, such as pretentious titles and epithets being applied to low persons, uphold the comic tone. Clothes imagery also points up the

key appearance/reality disparity.]

198   *THAYER, C.G. *Ben Jonson: Studies in the Plays.* Norman: Univ. of
      Oklahoma Press, 1963. Pp. 198-232. [Plot and subplot involve a
      direct contrast of two separate worlds which comment
      symbolically and contrapuntally upon one another: upstairs, a
      New Comedy world that mistakes appearance and reality;
      downstairs, all is disordered, bawdy, and absurd.]

199   *HAWKINS, Harriett. "The Idea of a Theater in Jonson's *The New
      Inn.*" *RenD,* 9 (1966), 205-26. ["All the world's a Play," as the
      Host tells us. *Theatrum mundi* is the governing metaphor, teaching
      an audience that by illusion—and all major characters assume a
      feigning disguise or attitude, being all the while Blackfriars
      *actors*—truths may be learned.]

200   CHAMPION, Larry S. *Ben Jonson's "Dotages": A Reconsideration
      of the Late Plays.* Lexington: Univ. of Kentucky Press, 1967. Pp. 76-
      103. [Not an attempt to reflect contemporary fashion, the play is
      instead a satire of the court's Platonic love cult and a parody of
      romantic comedy. Incongruous characters in both plots juxtapose
      true and false values.]

201   *DUNCAN, Douglas. "A Guide to *The New Inn.*" *EIC,* 20 (1970),
      311-26. [The play's subtitle, *The Light Heart,* points to a thematic
      concern: the inn is a *diversorium* (a "turning off" the main road), a
      place of "diversions" that include mindless brawling, sexual game-
      playing, and an asexual pastime, Platonic love; social
      responsibility is a related question.]

*Poetaster* (1601)

202   TALBERT, Ernest William. "The Purpose and Technique of
      Jonson's *Poetaster.*" *SP,* 42 (1945), 225-52. [Ovid's exile for
      licentious behavior is not *Poetaster's* essential plot, as O.J.
      Campbell has argued; rather, Jonson's formal design is
      continually engaged with aspects of one idea: the defense of true

poetry against its barbarous, malicious detractors.]

203 *WAITH, Eugene M. "The Poet's Morals in Jonson's *Poetaster*." *MLQ*, 12 (1951), 13-19. [Only partly satirical, *Poetaster* is a defense of poetry that stresses the poet's responsibility and moral obligations to society. Its structure enforces a contrast of virtuous poets (Horace, Virgil) as against the unworthy poet, poetasters, and Philistine detractors.]

204 *NASH, Ralph. "The Parting Scene in Jonson's *Poetaster* (IV, ix)." *PQ*, 31 (1952), 54-62. [When the ethically flawed Ovid parts from his beloved Julia prior to exile, height and lowness become thematic anticipations, in both verbal and visual terms, of a structurally important, later parallel (V.ii): Virgil's elevation in social status for true virtue.]

205 BARISH, Jonas A. *Ben Jonson and the Language of Prose Comedy*. Cambridge, MA: Harvard Univ. Press, 1960. Pp. 121-30. [Concerned mainly with Tucca as a Jonsonian triumph of projecting a character stylistically, Barish also sees the asyndetic, nearly connectiveless style as suggesting fixity of temperament, and egoism, among the characters generally.]

206 JACKSON, Gabriele Bernhard. *Vision and Judgment in Ben Jonson's Drama*. New Haven: Yale Univ. Press, 1968. Pp. 20-30. [No simple equation between bad ethics and bad poetry as in *Every Man in,* for poets and poetry may be effective in socially undesirable ways. Ovid, Horace, and Virgil form an ascending hierarchy of goodness defined by ethical utility.]

*The Sad Shepherd* (left incomplete; ca. 1612-1637)

207 *THAYER, C.G. *Ben Jonson: Studies in the Plays*. Norman: Univ. of Oklahoma Press, 1963. Pp. 247-66. [That pastoral need not be trivial is proved by this symbolic tragicomedy as it speaks seriously on art, nature, and human experience. Love and life, divided by

envious archetypes of evil (witch Maudlin and her devil), are
reunited by a poet figure.]

208    LERNER, Laurence. *The Uses of Nostalgia: Studies in Pastoral
       Poetry.* London: Chatto & Windus, 1972. Pp. 163-80. [Part of a
       chapter dealing with pagan-Christian syncretism in Milton and
       Herrick, the brief discussion of Jonson's work (pp. 172-77) stresses
       the ambivalent ties between the enemies of witchcraft, Robin and
       his friends, and its practitioners.]

## Sejanus His Fall (1603)

209    *ENCK, John J. *Jonson and the Comic Truth.* Madison: Univ. of
       Wisconsin Press, 1957. Pp. 89-109. [Lavishes high praise on the
       play for its verse ("tight and compact"), construction ("towers
       notably above its predecessors"), concept (tantalizingly
       complex"), and thematic imagery (rising and falling, light and
       dark, perverted sexuality, etc.).]

210    *NASH, Ralph. "Ben Jonson's Tragic Poems." *SP,* 55 (1958),
       164-86. [Non-Aristotelian and non-Shakespearean, Jonson's
       Roman tragedies are bold experiments deserving of a special genre,
       "tragic poems." Distinctive marks (scrupulous historicity, political
       morality, type-characterization) are fully considered, and
       *Sejanus*'s ethical imagery briefly noted.]

211    *RICKS, Christopher. "*Sejanus* and Dismemberment." *MLN,* 76
       (1961), 301-08. [When Seganus is vividly described in the last
       scene as having been torn limb from limb and beheaded by the mob,
       it but culminates scores of unflattering bodily images (faces, eyes,
       heads, tongues, hearts, etc.) symbolizing the wider
       "dismemberment" of the Roman body politic.]

212    *HIBBARD, G.R. "Goodness and Greatness: An Essay on the
       Tragedies of Ben Jonson and George Chapman." *RMS,* 11 (1968), 5-
       54. [At the play's heart is the irreconcilable, paradoxical opposition
       of two ideals: greatness (the historical truth) and goodness

(Jonson's moral persuasion). Deception, especially self-deception, is thematically important.]

213 *MAROTTI, Arthur F. "The Self-Reflexive Art of Ben Jonson's *Sejanus*." *TSLL*, 12 (1970), 197-220. [*Sejanus* so consistently stresses the artificial, hyperbolic, self-parodying qualities of its rhetoric, the play-acting nature of its actions, the role-playing bent of its personae, and theatrical motifs generally, that it affirms a deterministic worldview.]

214 EVANS, K.W. "*Sejanus* and the Ideal Prince Tradition." *SEL*, 11 (1971), 249-64. [Socio-political evils like materialism sycophancy, and despotism, which Jonson would forestall in Jacobean England, are mirrored in *Sejanus;* as against the ideal prince examplar, Sejanus the intriguing megalomaniac and Tiberius the vain tyrant are Machiavellian antitypes.]

215 *HAMILTON, Gary D. "Irony and Fortune in *Sejanus*." *SEL*, 11 (1971), 265-81. [Manifold allusions to Fortune and her effect on human destinies in the play do not make *Sejanus* an orthodox medieval *de casibus* tragedy; rather, Jonson employs the concept ironically, for real causality lies with human agents—Tiberius' manipulations and Rome's expediency.]

*The Staple of News* (1626)

216 *PARTRIDGE, Edward B. *The Broken Compass: A Study of the Major Comedies of Ben Jonson*. New York: Columbia Univ. Press, 1958. Pp. 179-89. [With didactic symbolism more obvious than in the major plays, Jonson once again depicts a world that inverts true values; money is sexualized and worshipped as a religion. Images of eating connote parasitic living.]

217 *THAYER, C.G. *Ben Jonson: Studies in the Plays*. Norman: Univ. of Oklahoma Press, 1963. Pp. 177-98. [Dominating the play is a social theme: the abuse of wealth and the distortion of values attending it—ultimately, a problem of appearance and reality. Avarice or

prodigality link everyone to the allegorical-symbolic-realistic
character, Pecunia.]

218    *CHAMPION, Larry S. *Ben Jonson's "Dotages": A Reconsideration
of the Late Plays.* Lexington: Univ. of Kentucky Press, 1967. Pp. 45-
75. [Departure from Aristotelian moderation in human conduct (as
in the prodigal and miserly Penniboys, and many minor
characters) organizes a play modelled on the Prodigal Son story,
itself a variation of the morality play.]

219    *LEVIN, Richard. *The Multiple Plot in English Renaissance
Drama.* Chicago: Univ. of Chicago Press, 1971. Pp. 184-91. [A
triadic relationship is formed by the society of "jeerers," the
Canters' College, and the News Office (institutions all allegorizing
abuses of language) which provides a coherent subplot for the
symbolic-realistic Pennyboy plot.]

220    *KIFER, Devra Rowland. *"The Staple of News:* Jonson's Festive
Comedy." *SEL,* 12 (1972) 329-44. [Many references
demonstrate that the play proper and its framing scenes are a
festive comedy, a pre-Lenten revel (especially for Pennyboy
Junior) of food, drink, raillery, and escape from responsibility. A
persuasive anthopological critique.]

*A Tale of a Tub* (1596-1633)

221    BRYANT, J.A., Jr. *The Compassionate Satirist: Ben Jonson and
His Imperfect World.* Athens: Univ. of Georgia Press, 1972. Pp. 160-
80. [New Comedy elements abound, including marriages; but the
latter occur in spite of the intrigue, not as its result. Organizing all
actions is nature's triumph on Valentine's day, when human
impulses overcome society.]

*Volpone* (1605-1606)

222    *BARISH, Jonas A. "The Double Plot in *Volpone." MP,* 51 (1953),
83-92. [In this valuable structural analysis, the Sir Politic-Lady

Wouldbe-Peregrine subplot is shown to have many links on the thematic level (ideas of mimicry, animality, folly, monstrosity, metamorphosis) with the main plot, whose actions are travestied in parallel and juxtaposed scenes.]

223　*PARTRIDGE, Edward B. *The Broken Compass: A Study of the Major Comedies of Ben Jonson.* New York: Columbia Univ. Press, 1958. Pp. 70-113. [Finds the reversal of human values at the play's heart, a fact symbolically expressed in imagery of animals, gold, classical mythology, religion, perverse sexuality, and eating— "The final food is man" (p. 107).]

224　*KNOLL, Robert E. *Ben Jonson's Plays: An Introduction.* Lincoln: Univ. of Nebraska Press, 1964. Pp. 79-104. [A beast fable, "The Fox Who Feigned Death," is the underlying archetypal action. Popular Renaissance bestiaries illuminate the characters' animal qualities which, with the other folkloric motifs, should take visual form. The "unnatural" prevails.]

225　*KERNAN, Alvin B. *The Plot of Satire.* New Haven: Yale Univ. Press, 1965. Pp. 121-42. [Acting is a pervasive and centrally important theme with associations of hypocrisy and deception; it is realized in theatrical language (scene, feign, mask, etc.), structure (the symbolic progression in Volpone's and Mosca's many disguises), and physical action.]

226　HAWKINS, Harriett. "Folly, Incurable Disease, and *Volpone.*" *SEL,* 8 (1968), 335-48. [That *Volpone's* world is a "hospital of the *Incurabili*" (V.xxi.120) is revealed by the thematic relationship between Erasmian folly and diseases/impairments (senility, deformity, fake and real sickness, etc.) that are incurable through false panaceas (gold, sex, Scoto's oil).]

227　*DESSEN, Alan C. *Jonson's Moral Comedy.* Evanston, IL: Northwestern Univ. Press, 1971. Pp. 70-104. [In showing the contemporary primacy of gold, Jonson uses means similar to those of the late Elizabethan moralities: e.g., in the main plot, three sets

of characters (the Virtuous, the Vice-like, and four social "estates")
provide morality-analogues.]

228    *DONALDSON, Ian. *"Volpone:* Quick and Dead." *EIC,* 21 (1974),
       121-34. [Objects to some critics' finding a hygienic morality in
       *Volpone:* virtue in Celia and Bonario is frail and relatively
       impotent; but vigorous, buoyant energy ("quick" is a recurrent
       word) lies with the amoral Volpone and Mosca. Yet, such life is
       offset by proofs of sickness and death.]

# Thomas Kyd

## *The Spanish Tragedy* (1582-1592)

229    *HUNTER, G.K. "Ironies of Justice in *The Spanish Tragedy.*"
       *RenD,* 8 (1965), 89-104. [Interprets the play not as freely-willed
       actions but as divinely predestined motions within a "dream-
       allegory" frame; this ironic mode of construction (watched
       watchers watching others) underscores the prevailing ignorance of
       all those subject to the justice machine.]

230    *BARISH, Jonas A. *"The Spanish Tragedy,* or The Pleasures and
       Perils of Rhetoric." *Elizabethan Theatre.* Ed. J.R. Brown and B.
       Harris. Stratford-upon-Avon Studies, 9. New York: St. Martin's,
       1967. Pp. 59-85. [Expertly shows Kyd's functional use of schemes,
       tropes, and figures (antithesis especially), which have both
       aesthetic and conceptual force in being integrated with patterns of
       action and structure.]

231    *COURSEN, Herbert R. "The Unity of *The Spanish Tragedy.*" *SP,*
       65 (1968), 768-82. [Secrets (both secret love and secret crimes)
       provide the key to structural unity, for either concealment or
       discovery is involved in all of the seemingly unrelated actions.
       Betrayals, not revenges, comprise an interior pattern of action
       imitated throughout the play.]

**Notes and Additions**

232    *BERCOVITCH, Sacvan. "Love and Strife in Kyd's *Spanish Tragedy.*" *SEL,* 9 (1969), 215-29. [Widely understood and applied in English Renaissance literature, Empedocles' cosmology stressed the opposition, alteration, and interaction of love and strife. This influences Kyd's structural pattern, plot-subplot parallels, character contrasts, and even imagery.]

233    BURROWS, Ken C. "The Dramatic and Structural Significance of the Portuguese Sub-plot in *The Spanish Tragedy.*" *RenP* (1969), 25-35. [Kyd included the Alexandro-Villuppo episodes "with deliberate intention of reinforcing and highlighting, not only the grief of Hieronimo, but his total dilemma and action" (p. 27). Counterpointing magnifies the irony.]

234    *MURRAY, Peter B. *Thomas Kyd.* TEAS, 88. New York: Twayne, 1969. [Filled with insights into the thematic import (viz., the love-hate affiliation, the inadequacy of *words,* etc.) of Kyd's elaborate formal parallelisms and his verbal and theatrical symbolism, Murray's scene-by-scene approach has flaws of occasional tautology and mere paraphrase of the action.]

235    *COLLEY, John Scott. *"The Spanish Tragedy* and the Theatre of God's Judgments." *PLL,* 10 (1974), 241-53. [Multiple playlets, pageants, and emblematic shows of arcane meaning occur throughout, providing analogies to larger events; but, as men perform cosmic drama on the "world stage," they—and we!—are baffled as to whether one is actor or spectator.]

# John Lyly

*Campaspe* (1580-1584)

236    BEST, Michael R. "The Staging and Production of the Plays of John Lyly." *ThR,* 9 (1968), 104-17. [A brief but illuminating discussion of how, by internal and external evidence, four major stage conditions of Lyly's plays may be derived which directly

relate to *Campaspe*'s interpretation: e.g., symbolic stage movements and exits at the right and left.]

237　　*SACCIO, Peter. *The Court Comedies of John Lyly: A Study in Allegorical Dramaturgy.* Princeton: Princeton Univ. Press, 1969. Pp. 26-94. [Structure, as independent anecdotes in series, and the play's euphuistic style are both partactic, unified in one definitional aim: to examine propriety as it relates to one's social role as king, artist, thinker, etc.]

238　　HOUPPERT, Joseph W. *John Lyly.* TEAS, 177. Boston: Twayne, 1975. Pp. 55-71. [In Twayne studies, discussions of individual works tend to be paraphrastic and comparative; Houppert is rather more analytical in this essay, stressing Apelles' love (not the king's) as the central element, and the shared limitations of statecraft, philosophy, and love.]

239　　WESTLUND, Joseph. "The Theme of Tact in *Campaspe.*" *SEL,* 16 (1976), 213-21. [Tact is a "sense of what is fitting and proper in dealing with others" (p. 213); it is thematic, in Westlund's usage, as a structural principle of character contrast: Alexander is ample in propriety, whereas the self-centered Diogenes and the self-abasing lovers are flawed.]

## *Endymion, the Man in the Moon* (1588)

240　　*HUPPÉ, Bernard F. "Allegory of Love in Lyly's Court Comedies." *ELH,* 14 (1947), 93-113. [Historical allegory aside, *Endymion* may be almost wholly explained in terms of love allegory: a psychomachy between earthly passion and passionless love. Allegorical personages, the comic subplot, and many emblematic details are interpretively relevant.]

241　　*SACCIO, Peter. *The Court Comedies of John Lyly: A Study in Allegorical Dramaturgy.* Princeton: Princeton Univ. Press, 1969. Pp. 169-86. [Endorses and extends previous commentary about the pertinent Biblical allegory (Ps. 85:10) of the Four Daughters of God.

The three dumb-show ladies (II.iii) are recalled (V.iii) to abet Cynthia's symbolical roles.]

242 *WELTNER, Peter. "The Antinomic Vision of Lyly's *Endymion*." *ELR*, 3 (1973), 5-29. [Weltner's anagogic rather than allegorical reading of the play, in terms of Jungian psychology, sees a matriarchal transformation-mystery as the central symbol: Endymion "moves" from Tellus (savage mother) to her antithesis, Cynthia (heavenly spirituality).]

243 SACCIO, Peter. "The Oddity of Lyly's *Endimion*." *The Elizabethan Theatre V*. Ed. G.R. Hibbard. Hamden, CT: Archon, 1975. Pp. 92-111. [Odd, because Lyly departs from his usual practices in staging and setting (the dreamlike unlocalization), characterization, and modes of action (narrative rather than anecdotal), the play is his Legend of Constancy.]

244 *GANNON, C.C. "Lyly's *Endimion*: From Myth to Allegory." *ELR*, 6 (1976), 220-43. [Renaissance allegorizations of the Endymion myth, set forth in Bruno's well-known *Gli Eroici Furori* and in works of other Italian Neoplatonists, explain Lyly's plots, character contrasts, and other structural elements, imagery, and particularly Cynthia's climactic kiss.]

245 *KNAPP, Robert S. "The Monarchy of Love in Lyly's *Endimion*." *MP*, 73 (1976), 353-67. [A rewarding exegesis of the play as a typological fable of fall and redemption, of heaven and earth rejoined, in which manifold meanings pose an enigma even as they unfold to analysis in terms of Renaissance emblems, mythography, numerology, dream theory, and herb lore.]

246 *LENZ, Carolyn Ruth Swift. "The Allegory of Wisdom in Lyly's *Endimion*." *CompD*, 10 (1976), 235-57. [First performed on Candlemas, the play is based on that day's Collect and liturgical readings in the Apocryphal *Book of Wisdome*. Because reality is perplexing and man's knowledge limited, only the Queen (Wisdom) can reconcile temporal/behavioral paradoxes.]

---

Notes and Additions

*Gallathea* (1583-1585)

247    LANCASHIRE, Anne Begor, ed. *"Gallathea" and "Midas."*
       RDS. Lincoln: Univ. of Nebraska Press, 1969. Pp. xxi-xxxi. [Of
       most value are remarks (pp. xxiii-xxvii) concerning form and its
       implications: "[Complex and ironic structural] interweavings,
       contrasts, and similarities define love and reality; and the
       definition is not simple, but all-inclusive."]

248    *SACCIO, Peter. *The Court Comedies of John Lyly: A Study in
       Allegorical Dramaturgy.* Princeton: Princeton Univ. Press, 1969.
       Pp. 95-160. [*Gallathea* is exactly analyzed for how its structural
       principles (analogy, juxtaposition) and its extra-allegorical notion
       of mythological "deity" relate plot and subplot by one formal idea:
       the defiance of divinity.]

*Love's Metamorphosis* (ca. 1588-1590)

249    *HUPPÉ, Bernard F. "Allegory of Love in Lyly's Court Comedies."
       *ELH,* 14 (1947), 93-113. [Argues that the play is a confusing
       hodge-podge unless read as a thoroughgoing courtly love allegory;
       one should find the mean between alternative extremes of conduct,
       severally personified: passionate changefulness on the one hand,
       or cruelty, coyness, etc.]

250    *PARNELL, Paul E. "Moral Allegory in Lyly's *Loves
       Metamorphosis,*" *SP,* 52 (1955), 1-16. [Lyly uses allegory
       playfully, exploiting in turns a character's symbolic and realistic
       traits. Excessive responses to love, whether affirmative or
       negative, are the bases for patterning all of the characters into
       elaborate symmetries of antithesis and parallelism.]

251    BEST, Michael R. "Lyly's Static Drama." *RenD,* N.S. 1 (1968),
       75-86. [Lyly's plays involve dramatic situations equivalent to
       paradox: a series of tableaux suspended in contradiction. Here,
       Ceres, embodying the opposition of fruitfulness and chastity, and
       Cupid preside over lovers in both plots who must be reconciled to

imperfection in love.]

252    SACCIO, Peter. *The Court Comedies of John Lyly: A Study in Allegorical Dramaturgy.* Princeton: Princeton Univ. Press, 1969. Pp. 161-65. ["*Omnia vincit amor*" (V.ii.13) supplies a fair epitome of the play. Cupid is its presiding deity, and his omnipotent amatory powers are diversely reflected in the several type characters—chastity, jealousy, lust, etc.]

## Midas (1589-1590)

253    HILLIARD, Stephen S. "Lyly's *Midas* as an Allegory of Tyranny." *SEL,* 12 (1972), 243-58. [The two major episodes, Midas' golden touch and his acquiring ass's ears, *are* connected, both deriving from Ovid. Lyly conflates the allegorizations of avariciousness and ignorance with the tradition of Midas as tyrant, stressing the political aspect.]

## Mother Bombie (1589-1590)

254    *ANDREADIS, A. Harriette, ed. *Mother Bombie.* ElizS, 35. Salzburg, Aust.: Univ. of Salzburg, 1975. Pp. 41-62. [Antithesis, so typical of Lyly's euphuistic diction, is akin to the contrapuntal, "situational" dramaturgy used here to examine three types of marriages—those of "love, labor, and grief." *Natural* and the *unnatural* are the wider concerns.]

255    WELD, John. *Meaning in Comedy: Studies in Elizabethan Romantic Comedy.* Albany: State Univ. of New York Press, 1975. Pp. 125-28. [Coherence derives from Lyly's "insisting that the play is about nature, law, and folly, or more precisely, about man's folly which leads him to violate laws of one sort or another." Words like *law, nature, fool* are key terms.]

## The Woman in the Moon (1590-1595)

256 HUPPÉ, Bernard F. "Allegory of Love in Lyly's Court Comedies."
*ELH,* 14 (1947), 93-113. [Two allegorical patterns govern the play:
Pandora's sequential domination by planetary influences
(Mercury, Luna, and five others) allegorizes a real woman as a
composite psychological entity; and Pandora's acting as part
symbol, part allegory of Woman Incarnate.]

257 BEST, Michael R. "Lyly's Static Drama." *RenD,* N.S. 1 (1968), 75-
86. [In Lyly's version of the Genesis myth, created woman takes
the form of the Eve-like Pandora; but in this Utopia, original sin is
the envy of the interfering planetary divinities. Imperfection in
love, ordained by those gods to be man's lot, is rejected for
martyrdom by Pandora's lover.]

# Christopher Marlowe

*Dido, Queen of Carthage* (with T. Nashe?; ca. 1587-1593)

258 ROGERS, David M. "Love and Honor in Marlowe's *Dido, Queen of
Carthage.*" *Greyfriar: Siena Studies in Literature,* 6 (1963), 3-7. [In
Marlowe's play, unlike its source in Virgil, the fulfillment of love is
incompatible with the pursuit of honor; Dido's passion cuts her off
completely from honor, which by contrast claims Aeneas' total
allegience.]

259 POWELL, Jocelyn. "Marlowe's Spectacle." *TDR,* 8 (1964), 195-210.
["Marlowe illustrates his theme with living 'emblems,' . . . concrete
dramatic images of the spiritual actions they describe" (p. 197). In
*Dido,* discussed on pp. 199-203, gestures, costumes, and props
ironically counterpoint the text, highlighting the compulsive
quality of Dido's passion.]

260 *GIBBONS, Brian. "Unstable Proteus: Marlowe's *The Tragedy of
Dido Queen of Carthage.*" *Christopher Marlowe.* Mermaid Critical
Commentaries. Ed. B. Morris. London: Benn, 1968. Pp. 27-46.
[Stylistically, *Dido* represents an experiment in court drama, a
sophisticated genre at turns spectacular, hyperbolic, lyrical, heroic,

absurd, with protean characters.]

261 ROUSSEAU, G.S. "Marlowe's *Dido* and a Rhetoric of Love." *EM,*
19 (1968), 25-49. [Marlowe the rhetorician assigns the appropriate
Aristotelian modes of persuasion to the respective defenders of duty
and love: Aeneas, in whom the figures of *logos* and *ethos* (reason
and character) prevail, and Dido, in whom figures of *pathos* (the
feelings) predominate.]

262 *GODSHALK, W.L. *The Marlovian World Picture.* SEngL, 93. The
Hague: Mouton, 1974. Pp. 38-58. [A thematic reading, also sensitive
to theatric expression, which explicates the "disruptive aspects of
love—the homosexual, the unnatural, the adulterous—those kinds
of love which... become personally as well as socially destructive"
(p. 56).]

*Doctor Faustus* (with S. Rowley?; 1588-1592)

263 *HEILMAN, Robert B. "The Tragedy of Knowledge: Marlowe's
Treatment of Faustus." *QRL,* 2 (1946), 316-32. [Faustus, the
"Everyman as Intellectual," hubristically wants science to do the
work of philosophy and religion, failing to see that knowledge-for-
power has limits. Analyses of the recurrent imagery and of the
structure scene by scene are integrated.]

264 *BARBER, C.L. "The Form of Faustus' Fortunes Good or Bad."
*TDR,* 8 (1964), 92-119. [Blasphemy is dramatized as a heroic
endeavor: perversions include iterative images of gluttony (also in
the subplot) which profane Holy Communion, and such corrupt
gestural substitutes for that ritual as Helen's kiss and the letting of
blood. A Freudian/theological reading.]

265 *HAWKINS, Sherman. "The Education of Faustus." *SEL,* 6 (1966),
193-209. [Faustus' "education" is his progressive initiation into
evil. A symbolic pattern recurs in the middle episodes which links
them to the climax: observation (all Seven Deadly Sins as abstract

pageant) and participation (ensuing concrete enactments of pride, wrath, sloth, etc.).]

266    *OSTROWSKI, Witold. "The Interplay of the Subjective and the Objective in Marlowe's *Dr. Faustus.*" *Studies in Language and Literature in Honour of Margaret Schlauch.* Ed. M. Brahmer et al. Warsaw: Polish Scientific Publishers, 1966. Pp. 293-305. [Conflicting interpretations of the play's meaning arise from a discord between two realities: subjective (what is thought, felt, desired) and objective (what really is).]

267    *SNYDER, Susan. "Marlowe's *Doctor Faustus* an an Inverted Saint's Life." *SP,* 63 (1966), 565-77. [Three "movements" work simultaneously: a morality pattern, promising last-minute repentance; a tragic pattern, promising a downswing due to heroic pride; and, reinforcing the latter, a parody of a half-dozen quintessential features of a saint's biography.]

268    *BLUESTONE, Max. *"Libido Speculandi:* Doctrine and Dramaturgy in Contemporary Interpretations of Marlowe's *Doctor Faustus.*" *Reinterpretations of Elizabethan Drama.* Ed. N. Rabkin. New York: Columbia Univ. Press, 1969. Pp. 33-88. [Cites eighty modern studies in arguing the play's interpretive ambiguity. Religious doctrine, as tested by genre, morality elements, comic episodes, and structure, is controversial; dramaturgy, especially as stage movements and positioning, is equivocal.]

269    *GODSHALK, W.L. *The Marlovian World Picture.* SEngL, 93. The Hague, Mouton, 1974. Pp. 169-202. [Profitably attuned to the symbolic nuances of theme (eating, transformation, dismemberment, etc.) and structure (sequent episodes as a progress to triviality), this reading stresses Faustus's degeneration. Cites from the widely accepted 1616 text.]

*Edward II* (1591-1593)

270     LEVIN, Harry. *The Overreacher: A Study of Christopher Marlowe.*
        Cambridge, MA: Harvard Univ. Press, 1952. Pp. 82-105.
        [Reconciling chronicle history with tragedy was the unique
        contribution of *Edward II.* Levin soundly distinguishes the main
        characters from those in the other plays, and offers thematic
        documentation of Edward's obsessiveness.]

271     *FRICKER, Robert. "The Dramatic Structure of *Edward II.*" *ES,* 34
        (1953), 204-17. [Scene-by-scene analysis indicates the play's
        structural unit to be neither episode, act, nor scene, but what may
        be called the "scenic section" organized into a rhythmically
        unified series of rapid, successive actions and counter-actions by
        the hero and his antagonist.]

272     LEECH, Clifford. "Marlowe's *Edward II*: Power and Suffering."
        *CritQ,* 1 (1959), 181-96. [Productions and criticism should stress
        "the thing that was most fully and persistently alive to the
        dramatist as he was writing" (p. 182): here it is the furthest reaches
        of human power, as it is bound up with the ultimate in human
        suffering—barbarous, humiliating, cruel.]

273     BEVINGTON, David M. *From "Mankind" to Marlowe: Growth of
        Structure in the Popular Drama of Tudor England.* Cambridge,
        MA: Harvard Univ. Press, 1962. Pp. 234-44. [Morality play vestiges
        (e.g., figural symbolisms, and a large cast to highlight the central
        four characters) clash with factual and character-drawing
        exigencies, making for ambiguity.]

274     STEANE, J.B. *Marlowe: A Critical Study.* Cambridge: Cambridge
        Univ. Press, 1964. Pp. 204-35. [In reply to critics who find no central
        theme or unity of tone, Steane avers that "the dominant spirit is one
        of belittlement,...the petty, undignified and humiliated are
        everywhere and this does make a distinctive tone or feeling" (pp.
        228, 230).]

275     *WAITH, Eugene M. "*Edward II*: The Shadow of Action." *TDR,* 8
        (1964), 59-76. [Frustration, resulting from disappointed hopes and

expectations, from manifold trammeling of wills, or from an inability to break out of some constriction, is the play's leading structural concept and its chief cause of emotion. Gesture and movement also embody the idea.]

276   *ZUCKER, David Hard. *Stage and Image in the Plays of Christopher Marlowe.* ElizS, 7. Salzburg, Aust.: Univ. of Salzburg, 1972. Pp. 114-42. [Close textual analysis supports a thematic approach rewarding for its novel emphasis upon Marlowe's iconic symbolism ("stage pictures"), as embodied in costumes, props, gestures, movements, lighting, decor, etc.]

*The Jew of Malta* (rev. by T. Heywood?; ca. 1589-1592)

277   LEVIN, Harry. *The Overreacher: A Study of Christopher Marlowe.* Cambridge, MA: Harvard Univ. Press, 1952. Pp. 56-80. [Self-interest and double-dealing prevail on the three interconnected and morally identical levels of plot: the overplot of power politics, the main plot of Barabas' peculations, and the underplot of Ithamore's blackmailing scheme.]

278   BABB, Howard S. *"Policy* in *The Jew of Malta." ELH,* 24 (1957), 85-94. [A recurrent pun on "policy," contradictorily meaning righteous public governance and private Machiavellian deceit, informs the central moral issues. Barabas' own hypocrisy makes him ignore the distinction, causing his downfall. "Profession" is another pun which underlines deceit.]

279   BEVINGTON, David M. *From "Mankind" to Marlowe: Growth of Structure in the Popular Drama of Tudor England.* Cambridge, MA: Harvard Univ. Press, 1962. Pp. 218-33. [In adopting the episodic structure of the mid-century moral play—aiming a Vice-like villain-hero towards a steady decline—Marlowe creates ambiguity by making God's avenger another villain.]

280   *HUNTER, G.K. The The Theology of Marlowe's *The Jew of Malta."* *JWCI,* 27 (1964), 211-40. [Modern anti-Semitism differs in kind

from the patristic-medieval *adversus Judaeos* tradition (which is theological, not racialist) relied upon by Marlowe, whose stance is ambivalently Christian, not atheistic, when he depicts Barabas as an Antichrist or ironic Anti-Job.]

281 *ROTHSTEIN, Eric. "Structure as Meaning in *The Jew of Malta.*" *JEGP*, 65 (1966), 260-73. [Structure and theme merge in the play's almost continuous use of a parodic technique that mocks romantic conventions like the code of friendhsip and the pastoral, as it depicts ironic analogues of such Biblical personae as Job, Adam, and the historical Barabas.]

282 *ZUCKER, David Hard. *Stage and Image in the Plays of Christopher Marlowe.* ElizS, 7. Salzburg, Aust.: Univ. of Salzburg, 1972. Pp. 80-98. [Noting that melodrama relies on intrigue, violent stage action, simple characterization, caricature, etc., Zucker sees this genre as underlying the play's emblematic unity of verbal and theatrical texture.]

283 *GODSHALK, W.L. *The Marlovian World Picture.* SEngL, 93. The Hague: Mouton, 1974. Pp. 203-22. [Expressing conflict between good and evil, the play is "bifurcated, built on doubles—on double characters, duplicity, double actions....On the imagistic and thematic levels, there is the contrast between...pretense and reality" (p. 221).]

*The Massacre at Paris* (1593)

284 STEANE, J.B. *Marlowe: A Critical Study.* Cambridge: Cambridge Univ. Press, 1964. Pp. 236-46. [Finds a resemblance to *Macbeth* in that conventional political and religious sentiments are presented not as concessions to popular prejudice, but as thematic evocations of the moral norm—a religious sense of God working and triumphing through Navarre.]

285 *ZUCKER, David Hard. *Stage and Image in the Plays of Christopher Marlowe.* ElizS, 7. Salzburg, Aust.: Univ. of Salzburg,

1972. Pp. 99-113. [No "loose succession of scenes, the play is structured effectively by contrasts between hierarchical order, weakly maintained, and the corrupt but vigorous forces of the Guise and Catherine de Medici" (p. 101.]

**286**    *GODSHALK, W.L. *The Marlovian World Picture.* SEngL, 93. The Hague: Mouton, 1974. Pp. 79-101. [Preceded by a reasonable assessment of the textual problem as it affects interpretation, this critique finds the play a structurally well-balanced study of religion creating means for political opportunism, and not even the pious Navarre is exempt.]

## *1 Tamburlaine the Great* (1587-1588)

**287**    DUTHIE, G.I. "The Dramatic Structure of Marlowe's *Tamburlaine the Great,* Parts I and II." *E&S,* 1 (1948), 101-26. [Tamburlaine's many conquests belong to a wider, coherent design in which Zenocrate is indispensable. As Beauty incarnate she inspires ambition (I.ii), later catalyzes pity (V. ii) to moderate, not abrogate his ideal of honor or *virtù.*]

**288**    LEVIN, Harry. *The Overreacher: A Study of Christopher Marlowe.* Cambridge, MA: Harvard Univ. Press, 1952. Pp. 29-54. [*Libido dominandi*—the protagonist's will to power, his boundless ambition in its most material aspect—unites both parts and dominates the verbal/visual stylistics: speech (including the manifold place-names), costumes, props, etc.]

**289**    *PEET, Donald. "The Rhetoric of *Tamburlaine.*" *ELH,* 26 (1959), 137-55. [Marlowe's use of Renaissance formal rhetoric is unique and functional. Virtually every scene involves exhortatory debating, and the myriad schemata and tropes of "amplification" serve not to magnify and provoke admiration for the protagonist alone, but for almost every character.]

**290**    BEVINGTON, David M. *From "Mankind" to Marlowe: Growth of Structure in the Popular Drama of Tudor England.* Cambridge,

MA: Harvard Univ. Press, 1962. Pp. 199-217. [Both parts of *Tamburlaine* derive their sense of form (episodic, linear, sequential) and their character patterns (psychomachic, symmetrical) from the earlier chronicle plays and moralities.]

291    WAITH, Eugene M. *The Herculean Hero in Marlowe, Chapman, Shakespeare and Dryden.* New York: Columbia Univ. Press, 1962. Pp. 60-87. [Marlowe's depiction of his own Herculean demigod, Tamburlaine, as an eloquent, wrathful, and cruel scourge of God corresponds to the traditional and, to him, familiar versions of Seneca and the Italian, Pollaiuolo.]

292    *ZUCKER, David Hard. *Stage and Image in the Plays of Christopher Marlowe.* ElizS, 7. Salzburg, Aust.: Univ. of Salzburg, 1972. Pp. 20-54. [Scrutinizes triumphal processions and tableaux which give emblematic form to the play's *de casibus* pattern. Theatrical symbolism often connects with verbal expression to produce distancing irony, complex responses.]

293    *HOWE, James Robinson. *Marlowe, Tamburlaine, and Magic.* Athens: Ohio Univ. Press, 1976. Pp. 39-85, 162-76. [Despite an exceptionable style, and a puzzling obliviousness of Marlowe critics who partially anticipate him (W. Armstrong, S. Snyder), Howe argues well that Brunoesque Hermeticism inspired Tamburlaine's and Zenocrate's transcendence.]

## 2 *Tamburlaine the Great* (1587-1588)

294    GARDNER, Helen L. "The Second Part of *Tamburlaine the Great.*" *MLR,* 37 (1942), 18-24. [Part II differs in intention and plan from the simply constructed Part I. Scene-by-scene analysis shows that the human will, so spendorous and implacable in the earlier play, is limited in its power by the resisting wills of others, and by inevitable necessity.]

295    DUTHIE, G.I. "The Dramatic Structure of Marlowe's *Tamburlaine the Great,* Parts I and II." *E&S,* 1 (1948), 101-26. [Whereas Beauty,

incarnate in Zenocrate, was Tamburlaine's partly victorious foe in
Part I (see V.ii.88-96), here Death proves a like adversary in taking
Zenocrate. Unifying all is the idea of the hero's sons as his martial
successors.]

296   *RICHARDS, Susan. "Marlowe's *Tamburlaine II*: A Drama of
      Death." *MLQ,* 26 (1965), 375-87. [Though Tamburlaine's death-
      dealing powers on the battlefield increase throughout the play, in
      his private fortunes there is a reverse process, a growing subjection
      to death that is at last fatal. All main actions are deemed ritual
      observances.]

297   *ARMSTRONG, William A. *Marlowe's "Tamburlaine": Its Image
      and the Stage.* Hull, Eng.: Univ. of Hull Publications, 1966. [This
      18-page essay, Armstrong's inaugural lecture at Hull, points up the
      Marlovian stage symbolism (costume, props, etc.) which augments
      the verbal sort: e.g., cabalistic fire/water imagery recurs as a
      Tamburlaine/Zenocrate equation.]

298   BARBER, C.L. "The Death of Zenocrate: 'Conceiving and
      subduing both' in Marlowe's *Tamburlaine*." *L&P,* 16 (1966), 15-24.
      [A "speculative" Freudian interpretation of Zenocrate's meaning
      for Tamburlaine (and indirectly for Marlowe): Tamburlaine, a self-
      made religion, is challenged by Jove's theft of his co-divinity,
      producing Oedipal feelings.]

299   *ZUCKER David Hard. *Stage and Image in the Plays of
      Christopher Marlowe.* ElizS, 7. Salzburg, Aust.: Univ. of Salzburg,
      1972. Pp. 55-79. [Stage pictures, involving more elaborate scenic
      devices (chariot, death-bed, hearse, etc.) than Part I, interact with
      verbal images to strengthen the ironic contrast between
      Tamburlaine's and Death's triumphs.]

300   *HOWE, James Robinson. *Marlowe, Tamburlaine, and Magic.*
      Athens: Ohio Univ. Press, 1976. Pp. 86-139, 177-80. [As in Part I, the
      Hermetic views and even the essential sun and moon images of
      Giordano Bruno are used, but are fitted to Part II's special dramatic

and philosophical problems: reconciling divinity-status with mortality, flux, and necessity.]

# John Marston

*Antonio and Mellida* (1599-1600)

301 *BERLAND, Ellen. "The Function of Irony in Marston's *Antonio and Mellida.*" *SP*, 66 (1969), 739-55. [Characters fooling themselves and each other form a world of deceit that is exposed, respectively in the main- and subplot, through irony and satire. Repeated contrasts of appearance and reality mock the heroism, thus parodying the romantic-comic genre.]

302 BERGSON, Allen. "Dramatic Style as Parody in Marston's *Antonio and Mellida.*" *SEL*, 11 (1971), 307-25. [Reads this play and *Antonio's Revenge* as a unified, ten-act drama; the first part establishes tragic atmosphere through psychically and ethically toned imagery (e.g., hostile nature, animals), and posits action/inaction as conflicting behavioral modes.]

*Antonio's Revenge* (1599-1601)

303 FOAKES, R.A. "John Marston's Fantastical Plays: *Antonio and Mellida* and *Antonio's Revenge.*" *PQ*, 41 (1962), 220-39. [Conceding there to be dramatic power and serious ethical intention, Foakes finds these qualities realized through a *fantastical* style—that is, the popular revenge play distorted by parody, bathos, and grotesque exaggeration.]

304 *FINKELPEARL, Philip J. *John Marston of the Middle Temple: An Elizabethan Dramatist in His Social Setting.* Cambridge, MA: Harvard Univ. Press, 1969. Pp. 150-61. [As cruel revenge transforms Antonio from one of sense to senselessness (inviting comparisons with his callous victim), imagery and chiaroscuro theatrical effects enhance the dark pessimism.]

305     *AYRES, Philip J. "Marston's *Antonio's Revenge:* The Morality of
        the Revenging Hero." *SEL,* 12 (1972), 359-74. [Antonio's private
        revenge of his father's death claims our sympathy at first, but after
        III.i ironic verbal and visual parallels with Piero the murderer, and
        the self-righteous use of religious imagery indicate a parody of the
        amoral Kydian revenger.]

306     GECKLE, George L. "*Antonio's Revenge:* 'Never more woe in
        lesser plot was found.' " *CompD,* 6 (1972), 323-35. [Stresses
        Marston's debt to Seneca's *Thyestes* and Shakespeare's *Titus
        Andronicus* for theme, style, tone, and emotional effect; e.g., the
        many references to blood (more than seventy) assert the idea of
        excess in *lex talionis* revenge.]

## *The Dutch Courtesan* (1603-1604)

307     PRESSON, Robert K. "Marston's *The Dutch Courtezan:* The Study
        of an Attitude in Adaptation." *JEGP,* 55 (1956), 406-13.
        [Malheureux internalizes the debate of passion and reason as
        Mankind, Franceschina assumes Dame Lechery's role, and
        Beatrice figues virtuous love in Marston's adaptation of the
        morality play, with its temptation-fall-redemption pattern.]

308     *FINKELPEARL, Philip J. *John Marston of the Middle Temple: An
        Elizabethan Dramatist in His Social Setting.* Cambridge, MA:
        Harvard Univ. Press, 1969. Pp. 195-219. [Details the unifying
        formal parallels and analogies, based on the contrast of natural
        virtue and specious purity, among the two plots and their respective
        characters. A gratifying study.]

309     *HAMILTON, Donna B. "Language as Theme in *The Dutch
        Courtesan.*" *RenD,* N.S. 5 (1972), 75-87. [In both the main plot and
        the subplot the central actions demonstrate how the irrational and
        foolish render language helpless, ineffectual; the quality of a
        character's speech is thus an index of his moral stature. Disguises
        aid social reform in both plots.]

*The Fawn* (1604-1606)

310 *FINKELPEARL, Philip J. *John Marston of the Middle Temple: An Elizabethan Dramatist in His Social Setting.* Cambridge, MA: Harvard Univ. Press, 1969. Pp. 220-37. [Inns of Court revels influence form and content, in particular the climactic mock trial where the satyr-satirist Fawn arraigns Gonzago (James I in caricature) for thriving on flattery.]

311 *KAPLAN, Joel. "John Marston's *Fawn:* A Saturnalian Satire." *SEL,* 9 (1969), 335-50. [The central actions are Duke Hercules' cleansing Gonzago's polluted court of its folly and unprocreative love, and ensuring progeny to sustain his own dukedom. Symbolically, he reenacts the mythic Hercules' Augean (satirical) and Boetian (saturnalian) "labors."]

*Histriomastix* (Marston a reviser? with others?; 1598-1599)

312 KERNAN, Alvin. "John Marston's Play *Histriomastix.*" *MLQ,* 19 (1958), 134-40. [Argues that the play is Marston's only, satirical, and unified; that apparent incongruities such as the silly Act II subplay of Troilus and Cressida and the Prodigal Son, and the jargon-spouting scholar Chrisoganus who becomes a railing satirist, are all evidences of breakdown.]

313 *GECKLE, George L. "John Marston's *Histriomastix* and the Golden Age." *CompD,* 6 (1972), 205-22. [A full cycle of the Wheel of Fortune is the structural idea behind the process of social breakdown, depicted phasally in the play's six successive acts. Chrisoganus' learning heralds the return of Astraea, figured by Elizabeth I, to renew the Golden Age.]

*The Malcontent* (1600-1604)

314 WINE, M.L., ed. *The Malcontent.* RRDS. Lincoln: Univ. of Nebraska Press, 1964. Pp. xvi-xxv. [Finds the play a virtual study in deception, with Aurelia, Mendoza, Bilioso, Maquerelle, and even

Celso among its practitioners; as deception's victim, Malevole uses
his role ("the mask-disguise is the central dramatic symbol," p. xix)
for self-defense.]

315    FABER, J. Arthur. "Rhetorical Strategy in John Marston's *The
       Malcontent.*" *HussonR,* 4 (1970), 18-24. [Discerns a structural
       pattern which enhances growing sympathy for Malevole and
       coincides with the modes of Aristotle's *Rhetoric:* Acts I-II (the
       deliberative mode, of politics), Acts III-IV (the forensic), and Act V
       (the epideictic, or ceremonial).]

316    *FINKELPEARL, Philip J. *John Marston of the Middle Temple: An
       Elizabethan Dramatist in His Social Setting.* Cambridge, MA:
       Harvard Univ. Press, 1969. Pp. 178-94. [Taking the wholly corrupt
       atmosphere for its cue, this essay would see all darkly: e.g.,
       Altofronto's malcontent is true, not a guise; he, Mendoza, and
       Maquerelle are kindred Machiavels.]

317    *JENSEN, Ejner J. "Theme and Imagery in *The Malcontent.*" *SEL,*
       10 (1970), 367-84. [Imagery defines characters and unifies the play,
       whose central theme is "the conflict between the forces of order and
       disorder, harmony and discord" (p. 380); heat and coldness, the
       bodily processes, rising and falling, and animals express courtly
       evil imagistically.]

318    *GECKLE, George L. "Fortune in Marston's *The Malcontent.*"
       *PMLA,* 86 (1971), 202-09. [Under Guarini's influence Marston
       adapts the Wheel of Fortune, the structural concept of *de casibus*
       tragedy, to the tragicomic form. A Christian pattern, it correlates
       Pietro's fall with Altofront's rise, and thematically distinguishes
       between Providence and Fortune.]

319    *SALOMON, Brownell. "The Theological Basis of Imagery and
       Structure in *The Malcontent.*" *SEL,* 14 (1974), 271-84. [Internal and
       external evidence attests to the Calvinistic worldview behind the
       play's imagery (sexuality, animality, scatology, *contemptus
       mundi*) and its archtypal structure, in which Malevole mediates the

natural and divine worlds.]

320    WHARTON, T.F. *"The Malcontent* and 'Dreams, Visions,
       Fantasies.' " *EIC,* 24 (1974), 261-73. [The playwright's fascination
       with the idea of role-playing gives special impetus to wish-
       fulfillment; the Genoese court fantasizes, creating "self-glorifying
       visions" (p. 262) of itself. Taxes Marston with contradictory, flawed
       character-drawing in Malevole.]

*Sophonisba* (1605-1606)

321    URE, Peter. "John Marston's *Scphonisba:* A Reconsideration."
       *DUJ,* 10 (1949), 81-90. [Mainly a descriptive appreciation of
       Marston's "austere and melancholy Roman tragedy," Ure's essay
       does weigh key antitheses, as the division of characters into the
       virtuous and vicious, and the running debate between Stoic
       morality and the need for public compromise.]

322    INGRAM, R.W. "The Use of Music in the Plays of Marston." *M&L,*
       37 (1956), 154-64. [Unusually full stage directions specify a wide
       range of musical effects in *Sophonisba* which are stylistically
       integral with the play's pagan framework, and which also have
       thematic implications (e.g., weird string music expresses the
       demon Erictho's evil love).]

323    FINKELPEARL, Philip J. *John Marston of the Middle Temple: An
       Elizabethan Dramatist in His Social Setting.* Cambridge, MA:
       Harvard Univ. Press, 1969. Pp. 238-53. [*Sophonisba,* Marston's
       quasi-Mariolatrous vision of a Stoic saint—of human perfection in
       an imperfect, expedient world—involves an abstract style, one of
       quasi-religious ceremony, sententia.]

*What You Will* (1601)

324    FINKELPEARL, Philip J. *John Marston of the Middle Temple: An
       Elizabethan Dramatist in His Social Setting.* Cambridge, MA:
       Harvard Univ. Press, 1969. Pp. 162-77. [Marston uses festive

revelry not as a healthy social corrective (cf. *Twelfth Night*), but as the stamp of an Epicurean world where one is initiated into unchecked, What-You-Will hedonism.]

# John Mason

*The Turk* (1607-1608)

325   *WILLIAMS, Gordon. "Image Patterns in Mason's *The Turke.*" *Trivium,* 9 (1974), 54-69. [At times, there is "thick-fingered obviousness" in Mason's method of painting a world of evil corruption in metaphors of disease, snakes, depraved or death-linked sexuality, etc., or through symbolizations of Medusa, Lamia, and Satan; yet it is a worthy first effort.]

# Philip Massinger

*Believe as You List* (1631)

326   GILL, Roma. " 'Necessitie of State': Massinger's *Believe As You List.*" *ES,* 46 (1965), 407-16. [Considerable first-hand use is made of Machiavelli's *Il Principe* to define the central ideological clash between Antiochus' humanitarianism and Flaminius' expedient statism. "Policy" and "politic" recur often, and though sinister are not without validity.]

327   *HOGAN, A.P. "Massinger as a Tragedian: *Believe as You List.*" *TSLL,* 13 (1971), 407-19. [Antiochus is repeatedly associated with Christ, while his tempter-adversary Flaminius, the personification of Roman tyranny, is a Satan figure. This full, sympathetic reading of theme and structure also explicates Massinger's use of theatrical symbolism.]

*The City Madam* (1632)

328   *LYONS, John O. "Massinger's Imagery." *RenP* (1955), 47-54. [The

play's dominant imagery involves clothes, a subject brought up no less than three dozen times (but particularly in IV.iv), and always with the implication that garments are not to be confused with true worth; Lady Frugal, her daughters, and the hypocritical Luke are the most clothes-proud.]

329 GROSS, Alan Gerald. "Social Change and Philip Massinger." *SEL*, 7 (1967), 329-42. [Massinger acknowledges the power of the trading class, but finds morally reprehensible examples—in the persons of Luke and the ladies Frugal—of its social and financial ambition, hypocrisy, and pride. Endorsed values are based upon hereditary prerogatives of the upper class.]

330 FOTHERGILL, Robert A. "The Dramatic Experience of Massinger's *The City Madam* and *A New Way to Pay Old Debts.*" *UTQ*, 43 (1973), 68-86. [Satire obtains almost purely here: Luke, chief purger of the world's folly (the medicinal image is repetitive), has himself a cureless viciousness. The habitual character-sketch technique also helps limit our sympathies.]

## The Duke of Milan (1621-1623)

331 LYONS, John O. "Massinger's Imagery." *RenP* (1955), 47-54. [Food and drink are the play's dominant images, and they serve as thematic metaphors to emphasize "the relationship between man's appetite for food and his appetite for sex....Just as lust leads to blindness and eventually revenge, gluttony results in satiation" (pp. 47-48).]

## The Great Duke of Florence (1627)

332 LYONS, John O. "Massinger's Imagery." *RenP* (1955), 47-54. [Images of a benign external nature—especially the seed which grows into a healthy flower (used seven times), and birds—are thematic expressions of the goodness, innocence, and healthiness of nature, as opposed to the wickedness and sterility of the court. Pages 48-50 deal with this play.]

---

## The Maid of Honour (ca. 1621-1632)

**333**    MULLANY, Peter F. "Religion in Massinger's *The Maid of
           Honour.*" *RenD,* N.S. 2 (1969), 143-56. [Religion is used simply as
           "the means to theatrical excitement and moving rhetoric" (p. 155),
           as are such other techniques of Fletcherian tragicomedy as
           structural symmetry, recurrent surprises and reversals, and
           conflicts of opposites like love and honor.]

## A New Way to Pay Old Debts (1625)

**334**    *LYONS, John O. "Massinger's Imagery." *RenP* (1955), 47-54.
           [Recurrent martial images (war, weapons, and military force)
           betoken the ethical contrast between the wicked, dishonorable
           Overreach and the virtuous soldier Lord Lovell and Allworth, his
           page. When both the latter use love banter, pleasant connotations
           are fixed upon martial terms.]

**335**    *BURELBACH, Frederick M., Jr. "*A New Way to Pay Old Debts:*
           Jacobean Morality." *CLAJ,* 12 (1969), 205-13. [With social morality
           in mind, Massinger updates the Prodigal Son parable in a morality
           play structure, making Overreach and his cohorts the Devil, the
           Vice, etc. The characters who embody Gratitude and Ingratitude
           divide along social class lines.]

## The Roman Actor (1626)

**336**    *DAVISON, Peter H. "The Theme and Structure of *The Roman
           Actor.*" *AUMLA,* 19 (1963), 39-56. [Form and meaning are indeed
           unified if one understands the play's allegorical concern with
           divine right—a burning contemporary issue. Domitian, the wicked,
           lustful, uxorious tyrant, is an "actor," like Paris, when he asserts a
           second, divine, identity.]

**337**    *THOMSON, Patricia. "World Stage and Stage in Massinger's
           *Roman Actor.*" *Neophil,* 54 (1970), 409-26. [The play "is unique in
           having an actor as hero, in containing no less than three plays
           within the play, besides other play-like scenes, in its use of the stage
           both as a figure in the action and as a figure of speech . . ." (p. 411).]

338 *HOGAN, A.P. "Imagery of Acting in *The Roman Actor.*" *MLR,* 66 (1971), 273-81. [Acting is an "architectural metaphor" which unites the two protagonists, Paris and Domitian, from the beginning of the play. Domitian and Domitia, deluded by the power-lust, merge reality and fantasy when they see life as a stage on which to enact their own ambitions.]

*The Virgin Martyr* (with T. Dekker; 1620)

339 *MULLANY, Peter F. "Religion in Massinger and Dekker's *The Virgin Martyr.*" *Komos,* 2 (1970), 89-97. [Religious ideas are prevalent in this tragicomic version of St. Dorothea's life and martyrdom—in the main plot's Christian-pagan conflict, in actual morality-play features (an angel and an evil spirit), and theatrically in costumes, movements, etc.]

# Thomas Middleton

*Blurt, Master Constable* (Middleton? T. Dekker?; 1601-1602)

340 *BAINS, Yashdip Singh. "Thomas Middleton's *Blurt, Master Constable* as a Burlesque on Love." *Essays Presented to Amy G. Stock.* Ed. R.K. Kaul. Jaipur: Rajasthan Univ. Press, 1965. Pp. 41-57. [Early critics misread the play as a true romantic comedy by ignoring signs that the genre was being burlesqued: viz., the witty, bawdy, hyperbolic style, recited by ultra-histrionic child actors in type-character roles.]

*The Changeling* (with W. Rowley; 1622)

341 *BAWCUTT, N.W., ed. *The Changeling.* Revels Plays. London: Methuen, 1958. Pp. xlv-lxviii. [Unifying links between the two plots are well documented. With moral contrast strongly implied, they take the form of imagery and diction (transformation, deceptive appearances, the labyrinth metaphor, etc.), and parallel actions which suggest deliberate parody.]

342    *RICKS, Christopher. "The Moral and Poetic Structure of *The Changeling." EIC,* 10 (1960), 290-306. [Five major words, the most important of which is *service,* have both a general moral application and a sexual one, and thus express poetically the play's key dilemma. *Honor, honesty, blood,* and *act* are the other puns, among whose cognates are *will* and *deed.*]

343    *BERGER, Thomas L. "The Petrarchan Fortress of *The Changeling." RenP* (1969), 37-46. [The play anatomizes the Petrarchan *topos* equating the beloved with a fortress and the lover with its besieger. Progressively, the literal and metaphorical aspects of the conceit are enmeshed in the main plot; in the subplot, the metaphorical becomes literal.]

344    *BERLIN, Normand. "The 'Finger' Image and Relationship of Character in *The Changeling." ESA,* 12 (1969), 162-66. [Verbally, but more especially in the form of theatrical actions (with props and gestures), the finger-ring-hand-glove imagery gives symbolic expression to the emerging physical and spiritual oneness of Beatrice-Joanna and De Flores.]

345    *JORDAN, Robert. "Myth and Psychology in *The Changeling." RenD,* N.S. 3 (1970), 157-66. [Beatrice and De Flores' relationship is a systematic travesty of the courtly love affair: the cruel mistress and the lovesick knightly champion; further, it echoes the wild man and the maiden literary model, which overlaps with the beauty and the beast myth.]

346    *LEVIN, Richard. *The Multiple Plot in English Renaissance Drama.* Chicago: Univ. of Chicago Press, 1971. Pp. 34-48. [Formal connection of the two plots is seen to be a negative analogy built upon direct moral contrast; in both there is sexual blackmail involving a heroine who must choose between fidelity or betrayal with a rival.]

347    *DOOB, Penelope B.R. "A Reading of *The Changeling." ELR,* 3 (1973), 183-206. [Sin—its causes, mechanisms, and consequences—

is the unifying concept of *The Changeling,* as much morality play as naturalistic tragedy. The Fall of Man is reenacted, imbuing characters, language, props, costumes, gestures, movements, and locales with symbolic meaning.]

## *A Chaste Maid in Cheapside* (1613)

**348**  SCHOENBAUM, Samuel. *"A Chaste Maid in Cheapside* and Middleton's City Comedy." *Studies in the English Renaissance Drama in Memory of Karl Julius Holzknecht.* Ed. J.W. Bennett et al. New York: New York Univ. Press, 1959. Pp. 287-309. [An appreciation of the author's "richest, most impressive" city comedy. Emphasizes the ironic view of pandemic corruption.]

**349**  *CHATTERJI, Ruby. "Theme, Imagery, and Unity in *A Chaste Maid in Cheapside." RenD,* 8 (1965), 105-26. [Discusses the family unit as the basis of thematic and structural coherence. Next, comic themes and attitudes are related to such significant image patterns as begetting and birth, animals, gold, the polysemous words "house" and "flesh," and others.]

**350**  *MAROTTI, Authur F. "Fertility and Comic Form in *A Chaste Maid in Cheapside." CompD,* 3 (1969), 65-74. [Fertility is the formal touchstone, allying the play's spirit to comedy's origin in phallic song; sexuality provides a corrective to asocial, life-denying behavior. Touchstone Sr. is a Priapus figure who changes funereality into festivity at the end.]

**351**  *PARKER, R.B., ed. *A Chaste Maid in Cheapside.* Revels Plays. London: Methuen, 1969. Pp. xli-lix. [Discerning a comedy of the grotesque that "modulates between several dramatic modes and relative moralities" (p. lix), Parker provides a detailed explication of its "ideas, actions, repeated words, and stage pictures, as well as imagery" (p. xlv).]

**352**  *LEVIN, Richard. *The Multiple Plot in English Renaissance Drama.* Chicago: Univ. of Chicago Press, 1971. Pp. 192-202. [A critical *tour de force,* equal to Middleton's remarkable achievement, showing how the four plots—each a sexual triangle—are arranged in order of descending importance and are elaborately interrelated, causally and analogically.]

## *A Fair Quarrel* (with W. Rowley; ca. 1615-1617)

353 BOWERS, Fredson Thayer. "Middleton's *Fair Quarrel* and the Duelling Code." *JEGP,* 36 (1937), 40-65. [Annotates the key problem of distinguishing truly valorous honor from foolish hardihood or mere quarrelsomeness in the main plot, which arises from Captain Ager's duel with the Colonel in accordance with the Jacobean duelling code's artificial punctilio.]

354 *LEVIN, Richard. *The Multiple Plot in English Renaissance Drama.* Chicago: Univ. of Chicago Press, 1971. Pp. 66-75. [Long admired only for its main plot (by Lamb, Swinburne, etc.), this tragicomedy is a sophisticated, integral unity of three levels. A basic formal connection is that all actions lead to a "quarrel"—a threatened duel over honor.]

355 FARR, Dorothy M. *Thomas Middleton and the Drama of Realism: A Study of Some Representative Plays.* Edinburgh: Oliver and Boyd, 1973. Pp. 38-49. [Focuses on genre mainly, placing this "hybrid," "transitional" play between earlier satirical comedy and the later, ironic *Changeling,* where as here truth and feigning ("false" recurs often) are thematic concerns.]

356 *ASP, Carolyn. *A Study of Thomas Middleton's Tragicomedies.* JDS, 28. Salzburg, Aust.: Univ. of Salzburg, 1974. Pp. 103-47. [Middleton internalizes Fletcherian tragicomic devices—disguise, dissimulation, and hidden identity—by transforming them into moral disguises of hypocrisy, self-delusion. Structure and imagery help intensify the moral enlightenments.]

357 *HOLDSWORTH, R.V., ed. *A Fair Quarrel.* New Mermaids. London: Benn, 1974. Pp. xxii-xxxix. [Thematic and structural

parallels among the three levels of plot action, one of them consisting of parodic clown scenes, are a major interest of this wide-ranging but compact discussion, which also posits Ager's Oedipal motivation and the function of noisy jargon.]

## *The Family of Love* (with T. Dekker?; ca. 1602-1607)

358    DAVIDSON, Clifford. "Middleton and the Family of Love." *EM,* 20 (1969), 81-92. [Middleton's satire is not aimed at Puritans in general, but at Separatists collectively and the Familist sect in particular—because of its presumptuous claims of unique piety, scorn of scripture and obscurantism ("darkness" being its metaphor), and sexual hypocrisy.]

359    *LEVIN, Richard. *The Multiple Plot in English Renaissance Drama.* Chicago: Univ. of Chicago Press, 1971. Pp. 58-66. [Structure consists in a three-level (romantic, satirical, farcical) hierarchical arrangement of the characters as to their relative importance, seriousness, and cleverness, and as to their sexual morality, since "love" is the issue.]

360    *MAROTTI, Arthur F. "The Purgations of Middleton's *The Family of Love." PLL,* 7 (1971), 80-84. [Purgation, a term making figurative use of the physiological theory of humours, is employed in this humours comedy as a metaphor for the satiric discomfitures of the morally diseased, as in the cases of Glister's and Lipsalve's lust, and Peter Purge's choler.]

361    McELROY, John F. "Middleton, Entertainer or Moralist? An Interpretation of *The Family of Love* and *Your five Gallants." MLQ,* 37 (1976), 35-46. [Middleton aims to entertain rather than to instruct: farce animates, though differently, all three structurally related actions. *Romeo and Juliet* and a score of popular conventions are burlesqued and parodied.]

## *A Game at Chess* (1624)

**362**    *SARGENT, Roussel. "Theme and Structure in Middleton's *A Game at Chess.*" *MLR,* 66 (1971), 721-30. [Spain's threat to England and her religion is the real subject: a dream-vision Induction frames the allegorical chess game, which is exploited in plot-subplot relations, ehtically toned imagery (black/white; the "discovery" motif), and by costuming.]

**363**    FARR, Dorothy M. *Thomas Middleton and the Drama of Realism: A Study of Some Representative Plays.* Edinburgh: Oliver and Boyd, 1973. Pp. 98-124. [Examines the play's two-fold nature through the characters, who while they primarily serve topical satire, also convey a frank, strongly felt moral aspect (e.g., in the White Queen's Pawn) new to Middleton.]

**364**    *DAVIES, Richard A., and Alan R. YOUNG. " 'Strange Cunning' in Thomas Middleton's *A Game at Chess.*" *UTQ,* 45 (1976), 236-45. [As chess is employed as the central metaphor, its traditional connotations (psychomachy, "game of life," nobility, virtue, order, transitoriness) fuse with new Machiavellian ones, producing moral ambiguity and satiric irony.]

*A Mad World, My Masters* (1604-1607)

**365**    TAYLOR, Michael. "Realism and Morality in Middleton's *A Mad World, My Masters.*" *L&P,* 18 (1968), 166-78. [Strong moral consciousness coexists with prurient wordplay and visual eroticism (e.g., the Succubus's temptation of Penitent, and Follywit's being accosted in his courtesan disguise). Comedy and cynicism participate equally, as sin is irresistible.]

**366**    *SLIGHTS, William W.E. "The Trickster-Hero and Middleton's *A Mad World, My Masters.*" *CompD,* 3 (1969), 87-98. [Follywit is a trickster hero, a character type whose forebears are the *adulescens* and *servus* of Roman comedy and the morality Vice. All three plots involve a wit-tricks-gull pattern, ironically unified by wrong motives' causing right actions.]

---

Notes and Additions

367 *MAROTTI, Arthur F. "The Method in the Madness of *A Mad World, My Masters." TSL,* 15 (1970), 99-108. [For satirical purposes, the titular "mad world" serves as a dramatic conceit: recoil, the principle by which characterological and situational extremes convert to their opposite, prevails. In several instances, reality is transformed into illusion.]

368 *LEVIN, Richard. *The Multiple Plot in English Renaissance Drama.* Chicago: Univ. of Chicago Press, 1971. Pp. 168-73. [The play's main action and subplot are both intrigue comedies, related by a formal analogy involving the equation of money and sex; moreover, the inter-plot equation is spelled out in the imagery as well.]

369 HALLETT, Charles A. *Middleton's Cynics: A Study of Middleton's Insight into the Moral Psychology of the Mediocre Mind.* JDS, 47. Salzburg, Aust.: Univ. of Salzburg, 1975. Pp. 63-92. [Approaches the play through Penitent Brothel, whose conversion reflects orthodox Renaissance psychology, and whose progress opposes that of Follywit in the main plot.]

370 *WIGLER, Stephen. "Penitent Brothel Reconsidered: The Place of the Grotesque in Middleton's *A Mad World, My Masters." L&P,* 25 (1975), 17-26. [Freudian psychology illuminates the play as comic-grotesque, a notion that embraces ambivalence and irreconcilability. Sexuality both amuses and provokes anxiety in us, especially in the Harebrain-Brothel subplot.]

371 LIEBLEIN, Leanore. "Thomas Middleton's Prodigal Play." *CompD,* 10 (1976), 54-60. [While exploiting the traditional paradigm of the Prodigal Son play, Middleton upsets its very assumptions: Sir Bounteous' flawed generosity makes him more of a true prodigal than his grandson, Follywit, whose acting of several roles in *The Slip,* etc. educates both of them.]

*Michaelmas Term* (1604-1606)

372   *CHATTERJI, Ruby. "Unity and Disparity: *Michaelmas Term.*"
      *SEL,* 8 (1968), 349-63. [Demonstrates the plot and subplot to be
      structurally and thematically unified: a Morality framework
      underlies the temptations and falls of Easy and the Country Wench
      in the respective plots. Actual and figurative disguises contrast
      appearance and reality.]

373   *LEVIN, Richard. *The Multiple Plot in English Renaissance
      Drama.* Chicago: Univ. of Chicago Press, 1971. Pp. 168-70, 173-82.
      [Plot and subplot are structurally equivalent, related by a formal
      analogy which involves both class conflict and the equation of sex
      and money.]

374   *COVATTA, Anthony. *Thomas Middleton's City Comedies.*
      Lewisburg, PA: Bucknell Univ. Press, 1973. Pp. 79-98. [Rites of
      initiation are at the heart of the play. Involved are the ability to
      distinguish real substance from accidents and false surfaces, and
      the opposition of parent and child in the maturation process.]

375   *HALLETT, Charles A. *Middleton's Cynics: A Study of Middleton's
      Insight into the Moral Psychology of the Mediocre Mind.* JDS, 47.
      Salzburg, Aust.: Univ. of Salzburg, 1975. Pp. 24-44. [Thematically,
      the alteration of innocence to sin takes substance in the city-
      country, appearance-reality contrasts, in the costuming, and in the
      clothes and feeding imagery.]

*More Dissemblers Besides Women* (ca. 1615)

376   *McELROY, John F. *Parody and Burlesque in the Tragicomedies of
      Thomas Middleton.* JDS, 19. Salzburg, Aust.: Univ. of Salzburg,
      1972. Pp. 106-54. [Counters romantic and naturalistic approaches
      to the play, showing instead that structure and texture are designed
      to parody romantic conventions of Fletcherian tragicomedy—
      Petrarchism, code of honor, etc.]

*The Old Law* (with W. Rowley & P. Massinger; ca. 1615-1618)

377 *ASP, Carolyn. *A Study of Thomas Middleton's Tragicomedies.*
JDS, 28. Salzburg, Aust.: Univ. of Salzburg, 1974. Pp. 148-210.
[Argues that the central situation of Evander's harsh edict is not
pessimistic, but an anti-realistic device permitting Machiavellian
natural law to create an "unnatural" anti-Utopia which only a
humanistic notion of law can undo.]

378 *ROWE, George E., Jr. *"The Old Law* and Middleton's Comic
Vision." *ELH,* 42 (1975), 189-202. [New Comedy conventions and
values (marriage, social harmony, renewal) are reduced to the
absurd, ironically distorted. By the "old law," the aged *die* when
youth triumphs! Extreme, discordant juxtapositions like
youth/age, good/evil, sexuality/death abound.]

*The Phoenix* (1603-1604)

379 *DAVIDSON, Clifford. *"The Phoenix:* Middleton's Didactic
Comedy." *PLL,* 4 (1968), 121-30. [Didacticism need not be
antithetical to art, for it is the basis of the play's unity: the
disguised Prince's educating travels (as Phoenix, symbol of
renewal) through his corrupt realm (cf. disease imagery) is a
creative discovery (cf. birth imagery) of good and evil.]

380 *DESSEN, Alan C. "Middleton's *The Phoenix* and the Allegorical
Tradition." *SEL,* 6 (1966), 291-308. [Middleton makes conscious use
of pseudo-allegorical techniques from the late-Tudor "estates" (e.g.,
Lawyer, Courtier) morality plays for didactic purposes. There are
half-allegorical personae with charactonyms like Fidelio or
Castiza, symbolic props, etc.]

*The Spanish Gypsy* (with W. Rowley [& J. Ford?]; 1623)

381 *BURELBACH, Frederick M., Jr. "Theme and Structure in *The
Spanish Gipsy." HAB,* 19 (1968), 37-41. [Shows that the play is a
coherent thematic and structural unity: the protagonists of each of
the four plots are, in varying degrees, prodigals whose regeneration
involves a paradigmatic journey into the gypsies' pastoral world,

and return.]

**382**    *KISTNER, A.L. and M.K. *"The Spanish Gipsy." HAR,* 25 (1974), 211-24. [Identity and its loss are the overriding and strikingly modern concerns in every plot-line: loss of selfhood and assumption of false identity are developed in symbolic terms by diguises, role-playing, verbal equivoques, veiled intentions, and the opposition of light and darkness.]

## A Trick to Catch the Old One (1604-1607)

**383**    *LEVIN, Richard. *The Multiple Plot in English Renaissance Drama.* Chicago: Univ. of Chicago Press, 1971. Pp. 127-37. [The three scenes featuring the hateful Satan figure, Harry Dampit, depict a "Usurer's Progress" from success to abject death. Contrasting with Witwood's climb to success, they supply a subplot analogue of the main plot's comic usurers.]

## The Widow (ca. 1615-1617)

**384**    LEVINE, Robert Trager, ed. *A Critical Edition of Thomas Middleton's "The Widow."* JDS, 56. Salzburg, Aust.: Univ. of Salzburg, 1975. Pp. xliii-lvii. [Comic protagonists move from disunity to unity, from singleness to marriage. This unassuming essay argues, "In *The Widow,* this movement towards marriage is blocked by greed, both for money and sex."]

## The Witch (ca. 1609-ca. 1616)

**385**    *McELROY, John F. *Parody and Burlesque in the Tragicomedies of Thomas Middleton.* JDS, 19. Salzburg, Aust.: Univ. of Salzburg, 1972. Pp. 155-215. ["Situations, roles, and moral sensibilities...are carefully, almost systematically juxtaposed; and, when taken in counterpoint, these elements express a single ironic vision of human absurdity" (p. 195).]

**386**    *ASP, Carolyn. *A Study of Thomas Middleton's Tragicomedies.*

JDS, 28. Salzburg, Aust.: Univ. of Salzburg, 1974. Pp. 211-57. [Self-conscious techniques of parody and burlesque anatomize tragicomic theatrical conventions (viz., the bed-trick and "resurrection" devices; ironic reversals) to discern serious ethical import: the equal illusoriness of lust and revenge.]

## Women Beware Women (ca. 1620-1627)

387   *RICKS, Christopher. "Word-Play in Women Beware Women." RES, 12 (1961), 238-50. [Wordplay has serious relevance to moral analysis in a play about the corrupting power of money. Among the words whose double senses exploit a connection between sexuality and mercenariness are "business," "employ," "use" and "abuse," "game," and "service."]

388   *RIBNER, Irving. Jacobean Tragedy: The Quest for Moral Order. New York: Barnes & Noble, 1962. Pp. 137-52. [Structurally, in both plots, the play is "a neatly interwoven series of moral choices" (p. 138). Highly developed iterative imagery and the element of ritualistic parody (the Ward's burlesque dance, the marriage masque, etc.) emphasize self-deception.]

389   *CORE, George. "The Canker and the Muse: Imagery in Women Beware Women." RenP (1968), 65-76. [Iterative image patterns contribute powerfully to the unity of action, feeling, and theme (love's failure in a corrupt society): disease and infection (the canker image predominates), blood, and feeding are among the clusters stressing the love-lust oxymoron.]

390   *EWBANK, Inga-Stina. "Realism and Morality in Women Beware Women." E&S (1969), 57-70. [Interlinked groups of characters form a structure whose interest is centered on social cross-sectioning rather than individuals, and on a pattern of perverted family relationships. Wit, in language and action (e.g., the chess scene), is thematically functional.]

391   *BATCHELOR, J.B. "The Pattern of Women Beware Women."

*YES,* 2 (1972), 78-88. [Emphasizes the play's binary formal symmetry: a diptych that affords mirroring versions— Venetian-Florentine, humanist-Christian, monist-dualist—of the same picture. Also notes five theatrical pageants, one in each act, which comprise a significant progression.]

392   MULRYNE, J.R., ed. *Women Beware Women.* Revels Plays. London: Methuen, 1975. Pp. li-lxxvi. [Though it falls short as an independent reading, Mulryne's essay helpfully reviews some bright but undeveloped explicative insights of others (e.g., M.C. Bradbrook and R.B. Parker), and is sensitive in its own right to Middleton's uses of visual symbolism.]

393   CHAMPION, Larry S. "Tragic Vision in Middleton's *Women Beware Women.*" *ES,* 57 (1976), 410-24. [Multiple plot lines converge on a single idea: manipulation of another for selfish, sexual purposes. Because the characters are morally obtuse and isolated, a fact conveyed by numbers of asides and soliloquies, the audience alone sees the evil objectively.]

*Your Five Gallants* (1604-1607)

394   McELROY, John F. "Middleton, Entertainer or Moralist? An Interpretation of *The Family of Love* and *Your Five Gallants.*" *MLQ,* 37 (1976), 35-46. [As with *The Family of Love,* some late revisionist critics also find this play a moralistic satire. Though its unifying idea (fellowship as impossible in an amoral world) is serious, a farcical tone prevails.]

# Anthony Munday

*The Book of Sir Thomas More* (with T. Dekker, H. Chettle, T. Heywood[?], & W. Shakespeare[?]; ca. 1593-ca. 1601)

395   McMILLIN, Scott. "*The Book of Sir Thomas More:* A Theatrical View." *MP,* 68 (1970), 10-24. [Matters of analytical bibliography— dust-dry but needful to prove theatrical coherence in this textually

disordered work—occupy all but the closing pages; there, props and furnishings of the play's six interior scenes are found to trace out a *de casibus* pattern.]

## *The Downfall of Robert, Earl of Huntington* (with H. Chettle?; 1598)

**396** MARGESON, J.M.R. "Dramatic Form: the Huntington Plays." *SEL,* 14 (1974), 223-38. [Margeson regards *The Downfall* and *The Death of Robert* as two parts of a single work, and he approaches the respective plays simultaneously; nonetheless, *The Downfall* is the more concretely examined for its use of Biblical symbolism, and play-acting as theatrical illusion.]

# Thomas Nabbes

## *Hannibal and Scipio* (1635)

**397** VINCE. R.W. "Thomas Nabbes's *Hannibal and Scipio:* Sources and Theme." *SEL,* 11 (1971), 327-43. [Over half the essay deals with sources—Livy mainly, and Plutarch for certain details; but the influence of Ciceronian philosophy (reflected in the thematic contrasts of passion and reason, private and public virtues) is second-hand from Petrarch's *Africa.*]

## *Microcosmus* (1637)

**398** *VINCE, R.W. "Morality and Masque: The Context for Thomas Nabbes's *Microcosmus.*" *ES,* 53 (1972), 328-34. [Morality play and masque elements are integrated into the overall structure: each of five acts comprises one of a sequence of iconic, tableaux-like "scenes" (Nabbes's word) representing stages in a temptation-fall redemption morality pattern.]

# Thomas Nashe

## *Summer's Last Will and Testament* (expansion of entertainment by J. Lyly?; 1592)

**399** *BARBER, C.L. *Shakespeare's Festive Comedy: A Study of Dramatic Form and Its Relation to Social Custom.* Princeton: Princeton Univ. Press, 1959. Pp. 58-86. [Nashe draws upon traditional materials of pageant and game—a festive lord and his court, with Bacchus as a Lord of Misrule—to turn summer-winter, holiday-everyday agons into serio-comic festivity.]

# George Peele

## The Arraignment of Paris (ca. 1581-1584)

**400** *LESNICK, Henry G. "The Structural Significance of Myth and Flattery in Peele's *Arraignment of Paris.*" *SP,* 65 (1968), 163-70. [Three elements constitute integral unity: the idyllic (Ida's Edenic beauty), the tragic (Colin's death, Oenone's betrayal), and the idyllic reasserted in the Queen's Christ-like redemption of paradisal glory by her rule.]

**401** *VON HENDY, Andrew. "The Triumph of Chastity: Form and Meaning in *The Arraignment of Paris.*" *RenD,* N.S. 1 (1968), 87-101. [The Renaissance masque is a formal exemplar: the prologue (Ate, goddess of discord) is antimasque to the masque proper (Paris' judgment in Troy reenacting the Fall and Redemption). Both episodes are analogues of Tudor history.]

**402** EWBANK, Inga-Stina. " 'What words, what looks, what wonders?': Language and Spectacle in the Theatre of George Peele." *The Eliabethan Theatre V.* Ed. G.R. Hibbard. Hamden, CT: Archon, 1975. Pp. 124-54. ["Wonder," denoting *admiratio,* "is the point of the whole play" (p. 137). The royal entry and submission ritual are its structural climax.]

## The Battle of Alcazar (1588-1589)

**403** EWBANK, Inga-Stina. " 'What words, what looks, what wonders?': Language and Spectacle in the Theatre of George Peele." *The Elizabethan Theatre V.* Ed. G.R. Hibbard. Hamden, CT: Archon,

tastes" (p. xxviii). Mainly impressionistic, this essay does comment upon unifying themes and images.]

## Hyde Park (1632)

413     LEVIN, Richard. *The Multiple Plot in English Renaissance Drama.* Chicago: Univ. of Chicago Press, 1971. Pp. 96-100. [Structured as a three-level hierarchy, *Hyde Park* features a symmetrical main and subplot, with another "half-plot" in a less serious vein. Initiating (and thus linking) all actions is a man's surrender of his loved one by compact.]

414     *WERTHEIM, Albert. "Games and Courtship in James Shirley's *Hyde Park.*" *Anglia,* 90 (1972), 71-91. [Games, competitive sports, betting, tricks, and trials pervade the play and are vital to the meaning and structural unity of all three plots (each of which depends on the defeat of a seemingly favored competitor); thus the across-stage footrace is symbolic.]

## The Lady of Pleasure (1635)

415     LEVIN, Richard. *The Multiple Plot in English Renaissance Drama.* Chicago: Univ. of Chicago Press, 1971. Pp. 99-102. [Structure involves an inversion of the three-level hierarchical formula: satirical exposure of the adulterous Aretina is enhanced by the contrast with "heavenly" Celestina and with Frederick, a burlesque version of Aretina.]

# Cyril Tourneur

## The Atheist's Tragedy (1607-1611)

416     *EKEBLAD, Inga-Stina. "An Approach to Tourneur's Imagery." *MLR,* 54 (1959), 489-98. [Scenes and incidents, reinforced by the imagery, are so patterned as to unfold a gradually progressing argument: evil is first postulated, then shown to work, and finally to self-destroy. D'Amville's hapless suicide is thus the play's logical

and moral denouement.]

**417** *LOVE, Glen A. "Morality and Style in *The Atheist's Tragedy."* *HAB,* 15 (1964), 38-45. [Antithesis is not only pervasive as a rhetorical trope, by means of which imagery, diction (the many puns), and syntax aid expression of the play's paradoxical vision, the device is also a controlling force with regard to the elements of plot and character.]

**418** *MURRAY, Peter B. *A Study of Cyril Tourneur.* Philadelphia: Univ. of Pennsylvania Press, 1964. Pp. 57-143. [Four perverted rituals, performed by D'Amville successively in Acts II-IV, give form to his rise and fall and relate to major image patterns (blood, house, flowing water, light/dark, etc.) and to key ethical contrasts among the characters.]

**419** *RIBNER, Irving, ed. *The Atheist's Tragedy.* Revels Plays. Cambridge, MA: Harvard Univ. Press, 1964. Pp. xxxii-lxvi. [Sees theme and structure as "built upon two diametrically opposed conceptions of man's position in the universe" and the ethical systems entailed by these conceptions. Summarizes criticism regarding imagery.]

**420** *KAUFMANN, R.F. "Theodicy, Tragedy and the Psalmist: Tourneur's *Atheist's Tragedy."* *CompD,* 3 (1969), 241-62. [Calvin's exegesis of Psalm 127 ("Nothing...without God's Grace") is dramatized. D'Amville interposes himself as a deity, freely using people as *instruments* of his *providence,* to *build* for his posterity (italics mark the key motifs).]

**421** *LEVIN, Richard. *The Multiple Plot in English Renaissance Drama.* Chicago: Univ. of Chicago Press, 1971. Pp. 75-85, 154-58. [Basic to the play's structural design is a three-level plot hierarchy, of which the first two levels are intertwined in a complex schematic and thematic fashion. Among the contraries and contradictories are reason and instinct.]

*The Revenger's Tragedy* (Tourneur? T. Middleton?; 1606-1607)

422 SALINGAR, L.G. *"The Revenger's Tragedy* and the Morality Tradition." *Scrutiny,* 6 (1938), 402-24. [The theme of a whole social order in disintegration is expressed through such morality conventions as allegorical characterization, disguises symbolic of moral transformation, sententious aphorisms, and by that icon of medieval attitudes, the skull.]

423 *LISCA, Peter. *"The Revenger's Tragedy:* A Study in Irony." *PQ,* 38 (1959), 242-51. [Tourneur's use of irony to objectify the underlying Christian moral order is intense and ubiquitous; it occurs both as action (the many ironic reversals in which evil multiplies, then cross-cancels itself) and as language (puns, personifications, and metamorphosis images).]

424 *MURRAY, Peter B. *A Study of Cyril Tourneur.* Philadelphia: Univ. of Pennsylvania Press, 1964. Pp. 173-257. [With transformation seen as the unifying action, this full exegesis treats plot structure as formally expressing that idea, Vindici's character in relation to total design, the moral allegory's strong medieval flavor, and verbal symbolism.]

425 *WIGLER, Stephen. "If Looks Could Kill: Fathers and Sons in *The Revenger's Tragedy." CompD,* 9 (1975), 206-25. [In this convincing Freudian reading, iterated eye/sight images are linked to sexuality and violence; blinding to murder and castration; swords to phallicism. Incestuous rivalry extends to every main character, evoking Oedipal feelings in us.]

426 *WILDS, Nancy G. " 'Of Rare Fire Compact': Image and Rhetoric in *The Revenger's Tragedy." TSLL,* 17 (1975), 61-74. [Imagery expresses vividly the play's vice and disorder in sensuous terms (the head being the controlling motif), but also of moral and aesthetic importance are rhetorical schemata, tropes, and devices like antithesis, paradox, and oxymoron.]

**427**  *BARISH, Jonas A. "The True and False Families of *The Revenger's Tragedy." English Renaissance Drama: Essays in Honor of Madeleine Doran & Mark Eccles.* Ed. S. Henning et al. Carbondale: Southern Illinois Univ. Press, 1976. Pp. 142-54. [Hardened by revenge though Vindice and Hippolito are, they and their mother and sister comprise a close moral unit; but the evil ducal family is splintered by competing appetites.]

**428**  *PEARCE, Howard. *"Virtù and Poesis in The Revenger's Tragedy." ELH,* 43 (1976), 19-37. [Almost every character in the play is an artist—a virtuoso performer, a "maker"—who uses the arts of rhetoric and drama with creative force (*virtù*) for self-fulfillment, though to uncertain ends. Thus, images of art and skill stand opposed to corruption and decay.]

## John Webster

*Appius and Virginia* (with T. Heywood?; ca. 1625-1627)

**429**  EKEBLAD, Inga-Stina. "Storm Imagery in *Appius and Virginia." N&Q,* N.S. 3 (1956), 5-7. [Storm imagery creates a sense of tense foreboding, as in *The Duchess of Malfi,* strengthening Webster's claims to authorship. More important, "Images and plot-movement are closely interrelated; each single image depends for its meaning" on past, present, future actions.]

*A Cure for a Cuckold* (with W. Rowley & T. Heywood [?]; 1624-ca. 1625)

**430**  *MURRAY, Peter B. *A Study of John Webster.* SEngL, 50. The Hague: Mouton, 1969. Pp. 215-36. [Both plots, unified by analogies and contrasts, appose different kinds of love and friendship to prove that mutual forgiveness "cures" our corrupted wills. Compass is the central metaphor (cf. path, labyrinth, riddle), supported by death/rebirth and key/lock.]

*The Devil's Law Case* (1610-1619)

431    GUNBY, D.C. *"The Devil's Law-Case:* An Interpretation." *MLR,* 63
       (1968), 545-58. [While it is temptingly easy to regard it as a tragedy
       *manque,* the play makes use of tragicomic formal elements
       (mystification, improbability, etc.) and its didactically directed plot
       and characters to produce a thesis play having a controlling
       attitude to life.]

432    *MURRAY, Peter B. *A Study of John Webster.* SEngL, 50. The
       Hague: Mouton, 1969. Pp. 185-214. [Actions reinforce a theological
       idea: God's hand alone intervenes to save humanity from its evil.
       Evil is manifest in the repeated clashes between empty human
       words and life-and-death events, and in the fact that one profession
       (medicine, etc.) is exposed in each of the five acts.]

433    *BERRY, Ralph. *The Art of John Webster.* Oxford: Clarendon Press,
       1972. Pp. 151-67 et passim. [An act-by-act reading of the work as
       "above all an analysis of social evil.... Evil here is related to gold,
       the mainspring of social wrong. The Law in all its aspects [divine,
       natural, civil] confronts, but can at the end only rebuke this evil"
       (p. 167).]

## *The Duchess of Malfi* (1612-1614)

434    *EKEBLAD, Inga-Stina. "The 'Impure Art' of John Webster." *RES,*
       9 (1958), 253-67. ["Impure art" is T.S. Eliot's critique of Webster's
       mix of realism with unrealistic conventions. Ekeblad, however,
       proves IV.ii's thematic import and structure, being a five-part
       paradigm of an Elizabethan marriage masque, with the madmen
       as an antimasque of *dis*unity.]

435    *CALDERWOOD, James L. *"The Duchess of Malfi:* Styles of
       Ceremony." *EIC,* 12 (1962), 133-47. [Ceremony and ritual, the
       symbolic forms of order, dramatize the tension between societal
       norms (specifically, Degree as a religio-political doctrine) and
       private impulse. Crucial scenes include the Duchess' courtship and
       the purgation ritual that is her death.]

**436** *KNIGHT, G. Wilson. *"The Duchess of Malfi." MHRev,* 4 (1967), 88-113. [Wilson Knight's mastery of the stylistic field approach to interpretation is well known from his books on Shakespeare. Here, some two-dozen imagistic and symbolic clusters—texture thicker that Shakespeare's—convey finally the impression that the forces of death are self-negating.]

**437** *GIANETTI, Louis D. "A Contemporary View of *The Duchess of Malfi." CompD,* 3 (1969), 297-307. [Buttresses an interpretive concept of the play with proofs that Webster, like Harold Pinter and Samuel Beckett, imparts key ideas and emotions by such nonverbal means as spatial positioning, lighting, decor, props, costume, make-up, and even vocal noises.]

**438** *MURRAY, Peter B. *A Study of John Webster.* SEngL, 50. The Hague: Mouton, 1969. Pp. 118-84. [Both the Duchess and Antonio affirm the values of goodness and true greatness found in Christian-Stoic integrity (patterns evoking Job, the Virgin, and the Holy Family support this idea). Bosola and Ferdinand—two Tantaluses—are well analyzed in Freudian terms.]

**439** *GUNBY, D.C. *"The Duchess of Malfi:* a Theological Approach." *John Webster.* Ed. B. Morris. Mermaid Critical Commentaries. London: Benn, 1970. Pp. 181-204. [Imagery, action, and figural symbolisms define the work not as existentialist but rather as exemplifying theodicy—the worldview of didactic, fideistic, providence-affirming Jacobean Anglicanism.]

**440** *BERRY, Ralph. *The Art of John Webster.* Oxford: Clarendon Press, 1972. Pp. 107-50 et passim. [Having previously established Webster's technique as that of the Baroque epoch style (sensationalism, parody, death-obsession, etc.), Berry finely analyzes three major themes and their metaphors, and also examines Bosola and the Duchess in existential terms.]

*The White Devil* (1609-1612)

441    BOGARD, Travis. *The Tragic Satire of John Webster*. Berkeley: Univ. of California Press, 1955. Pp. 117-28 et passim. ["Courtly reward / And punishment" (I.i.3-4) is the controlling idea. From that bitter speech of Lodovico's at its start until Vittoria's dying words (V.vi.261-62), the play teems with examples of the court's corruption and treachery.]

442    LAYMAN, B.J. "The Equilibrium of Opposites in *The White Devil.*" *PMLA,* 74 (1959), 336-47. [A characterological study of the leading figures, Vittoria and her brother Flamineo, that finds their paradoxical relationship central in structuring a complex response to a violent, fraudulent world: he diseased, repellent; she healthy, attractive, etc.]

443    *HURT, James R. "Inverted Rituals in Webster's *The White Devil.*" *JEGP,* 61 (1962), 42-47. [Rites of marriage, confession, and extreme unction are three religious rituals which appear in inverted, parodistic form. Like the other visual "figures-in-action," and the linking of characters with witches and devils, they relate fair show and foul truth.]

444    *MURRAY, Peter B. *A Study of John Webster*. SEngL, 50. The Hague: Mouton, 1969. Pp. 31-117. [Stresses metaphoric resonances of the white devil *topos* (vice hiding as virtue), which applies to nearly every character and not simply Vittoria. Other imagery, structural parallels, and morality play figural symbolisms are worked into the discussion.]

445    *BERRY, Ralph. *The Art of John Webster*. Oxford: Clarendon Press, 1972. Pp. 83-106 et passim. [Initial chapters develop a strong case for grounding Webster's dramatic ideas and technique in the Baroque period style, whose thematic and aesthetic concerns (naturalism, sensationalism) then underpin a full analysis of the play's metaphors for human evil.]

446    *SCHUMAN, Samuel. "The Ring and the Jewel in Webster's Tragedies." *TSLL,* 14 (1972), 253-68. [Sexual relationships play an

---

important role, as do the hand props that recurrently symbolize them: jewels and rings mock the institution of marriage (especially in the sequent rituals of I.ii and II.i) and provide interconnections among the four principals.]

**447**    *HOLLAND, George. "The Function of the Minor Characters in *The White Devil." PQ,* 52 (1973), 43-54. [Monticelso, Isabella, Lodovico, Francisco, Cornelia, and Giovanni are minor characters, yet help unify the play's circular structure: corruption spreads by example from individual to family, to society, thence back to its originator, destroying all.]

# Anonymous Plays

*Arden of Feversham* (T. Kyd?; 1585-1592)

448    CHAPMAN, Raymond. *"Arden of Faversham:* Its Interest Today."
         *English,* 11 (1956), 15-17. [Interest lies in socio-economic parallels
         to the disintegrations of our own parlous times: Arden is a "new"
         landowner whom Greene and Reede resent; the Ardens and Mosby,
         the rich, one-time tailor, are bourgeois snobs; and Black Will and
         Shakebag are "modern" thugs.]

449    *YOUNGBLOOD, Sarah. "Theme and Imagery in *Arden of
         Feversham." SEL,* 3 (1963), 207-18. [As all genuine tragedy depicts
         violations of the moral order with tragic human consequences, so
         with *Arden,* wherein evil is expressed through imagery of perverted
         religion, blood, light opposed to darkness (also reinforced
         structurally), and anarchic nature.]

450    *BLUESTONE, Max. "The Imagery of Tragic Melodrama in *Arden
         of Feversham." DramS,* 5 (1966), 171-81. [Conspiracy, pursuit,
         doubtfulness, torment, and capture are ways of life in a world
         askew: in imagistic terms, the human body is lacerated, violated;
         natural growth and generation are blighted, infertile, suggesting
         an inversion of the vegetation myth.]

451    *MARSDEN, Michael T. "The Otherworld of *Arden of Feversham."*

*SFQ,* 36 (1972), 36-42. [Numerous folk motifs and beliefs (e.g., the curse, crucifix, dream vision, number three) are functional in the play, establishing the influence of the supernatural "otherworld" upon the natural world of Elizabethan England.]

452   *WINE, M.L., ed. *The Tragedy of Master Arden of Faversham.* Revels Plays. London: Methuen, 1973. Pp. lvii-lxxxi. [Assesses *Arden*'s unifying ideas (e.g., "Covetousness—of land, money, social position, revenge, other people—motivates almost every character," p. lxiv), which are expressed through its texture and repetitive, incremental structural design.]

453   *OUSBY, Ian and Heather Dubrow. "Art and Language in *Arden of Faversham.*" *DUJ,* 36 (1975), 47-54. [Use and abuse of language signal moral disorder: e.g., Alice's and Mosby's manipulative rhetoric is parodied in Michael's euphuistic love letter; hyperbolic threats, oaths, and fantasizing reflect psychological breakdown in the various conspirators.]

## *Edward III* (W. Shakespeare in part?; ca. 1590-1595)

454   *KOSKENNIEMI, Inna. "Themes and Imagery in *Edward III.*" *NM,* 65 (1964), 446-80. [Education is the unifying prinicple: the King must subdue his adulterous passion for the Countess of Salisbury, the Black Prince must gain self-reliance in battle. Relevent image patterns include those of *law, marriage, animals, poison,* and the duple-connotative *sun* and *warfare.*]

## *A Knack to Know a Knave* (W. Kempe? G. Peele? R. Wilson?; 1592)

455   HOUSER, David J. "Purging the Commonwealth: Marston's Disguised Dukes and *A Knack to Know a Knave.*" *PMLA,* 89 (1974), 993-1006. [Overplot and subplot are analogous: King Edgar's uncovering Ethenwald's knavery matches Honesty's ferreting out vices in several social-"estates" characters. The disguised-spy figure anticipates Marston's Fawnus and Malevole.]

*The Life and Death of Jack Straw* (1590-1593)

456 ADKINS, Mary Grace Muse. "A Theory About *The Life and Death of Jack Straw."Studies in English* (Univ. of Texas), 28 (1949), 57-82. [From historical evidence two important significances to its contemporary audience are theorized for *Jack Straw*: that the Peasants' Revolt facing Richard II mirrored Elizabethan social stresses, and that the flattering depiction of a virtuous Richard had Elizabeth as a model.]

*The Second Maiden's Tragedy* (T. Middleton? C. Tourneur?; 1611)

457 *LEVIN, Richard. *The Multiple Plot in English Renaissance Drama.* Chicago: Univ. of Chicago Press, 1971. Pp. 25-34. [Plot and subplot are formally related by direct contrast of the respective plots' heroines. An overall analogy with aspects both spatial and temporal—viz., scenic sequence—is set up to exploit moral differences between the two plots.]

458 LANCASHIRE, Anne. "*The Second Maiden's Tragedy*: A Jacobean Saint's Life." *RES,* 25 (1974), 267-79. [Because the most important source of the main plot, in which the Lady chooses heroic suicide over the Tyrant's lust, is determined to be a Christian martyr's-life (that of Sophronia), a generic basis exists for details pointing to the Lady as a Christ figure.]

*A Warning for Fair Women* (T. Heywood?; ca. 1598-1599)

459 CANNON, Charles Dale, ed. *"A Warning for Fair Women"*: A *Critical Edition.* SEngL, 86. The Hague: Mouton, 1975. Pp. 48-91. [Treated at length are domestic tragedy as genre, the play's source, and extant commentary, but the section devoted to staging (pp. 48-58) is the most suggestive for interpretation—especially the stress on symbolic darkness.]

*Wit's Triumvirate* (1635)

---

Notes and Additions

**460**   *NELSON, Cathryn Anne, ed. *A Critical Edition of "Wit's Triumvirate, or The Philosopher."* JDS, 57. 2 vols. Salzburg, Aust.: Univ. of Salzburg, 1975. I, 1-43. [Technique, incidents, and relationships are indebted to Jonson's *Alchemist*. Realistic confidence men and gulls interact with the morality's allegorical mode to assert the right use of knowledge.]

# Masques, Entertainments, Pageants

## NICHOLAS BRETON (1545?-1626?)

*The Entertainment at Elvetham* (with G. Buc & T. Watson?; 20-23 Sept. 1591)

**461**    BOYLE, Harry H. "Elizabeth's Entertainment at Elvetham: War Policy in Pageantry." *SP,* 68 (1971), 146-66. [Not the usual form of entertainment (that is, unconnected units of pageantry), this spectacular outdoor water-show utilizes a dialectical mimesis (view-counterview-resolution) to figure forth topical allegory about the Anglo-Spanish War.]

## GEORGE CHAPMAN

*The Masque of the Middle Temple and Lincoln's Inn* (15 Feb. 1613)

**462**    *REESE, Jack E. "Unity in Chapman's *Masque of the Middle Temple and Lincoln's Inn.*" *SEL,* 4 (1964), 291-305. [Married love becomes a microcosm of divine love through several unifying dramatic motifs, such as the circle, the union of the Old and New Worlds, mythological marriages of heaven and earth, and the Neoplatonic allegory of love and beauty.]

**463**  GORDON, D.J. "Chapman's *Memorable Masque.*" *The Renaissance Imagination: Essays and Lectures by D.J. Gordon.* Ed. S. Orgel. Berkeley: Univ. of California Press, 1975. Pp. 194-202. [Reconciliation of opposites is the key: wealth and fortune, severally, with honor and virtue. Hitherto unpublished in English, this 1956 essay appeared first in French.]

## SAMUEL DANIEL (1563-1619)

*The Vision of the Twelve Goddesses* (8 Jan. 1604)

**464**  *CREIGH, Geoffrey. "Samuel Daniel's Masque *The Vision of the Twelve Goddesses.*" *E&S*, 34 (1971), 22-35. [Daniel's theory of masque is self-consistent and sophisticated, but unlike Jonson's, it gives priority to the visual over the verbal function. Emblematic goddess-masquers are as much personations of Platonic Ideas as the mythological originals.]

## WILLIAM DAVENANT

*Salmacida Spolia* (21 Jan. 1640)

**465**  GORDON, D.J. "Roles and Mysteries." *The Renaissance Imagination: Essays and Lectures by D.J. Gordon.* Ed. S. Orgel. Berkeley: Univ. of California Press, 1975. Pp. 3-23. [That the masque's allegorical iconography is shown to derive from Rubens' ceiling paintings at the Whitehall Banqueting House is of signal importance, as are the hermetic implications.]

## FRANCIS DAVISON (ca. 1575-ca. 1621)

*The Masque of Proteus and the Rock Adamantine* (with T. Campion; 3 Mar. 1595)

**466**  ORGEL, Stephen. *The Jonsonian Masque.* Cambridge, MA: Harvard Univ. Press, 1965. Pp. 8-18. [Davison's late-Elizabethan masque is seen a prototypical of Jonson's received tradition. Proteus, an embryonic antimasque, champions literal reality—the lodestone Rock—whereas the Esquire proves the superior, spiritual "attractiveness" of the royal guest.]

# THOMAS DEKKER

*Troia Nova Triumphans* (29 Oct. 1612)

**467**  *BERGERON, David M. *English Civic Pageantry 1558-1642.* Columbia: Univ. of South Carolina Press, 1971. Pp. 163-70. [Dekker's first mayoral pageant, one of the century's most expensive, is a coherent dramatic action whose form (conflict with evil/vision/salvation) resembles the morality play pattern and involves the Lord Mayor as an active participant.

# JOHN FORD

*The Sun's Darling* (with T. Dekker; 1624)

**468**  STAVIG, Mark. *John Ford and the Traditional Moral Order.* Madison: Univ. of Wisconsin Press, 1968. Pp. 49-54. [Man's pilgrimage of life is rehearsed in the masque's allegorical structure: successively encountering Spring, Summer, and Autumn, Raybright (everyman) spurns their country delights. Finally, the Sun brings reformation in sage Winter's court.]

# BEN JONSON

*The Golden Age Restored* (6 Jan. 1615)

**469**    FURNISS, W. Todd. "Ben Jonson's Masques." *Three Studies in the Renaissance: Sidney, Jonson, Milton.* New Haven: Yale Univ. Press, 1958. Pp. 119-24. [Gold-mineral-money images miltiply throughout the progress of this masque, which deals with Astraea's descending, at the request of Pallas, to supplant the Iron Age with the Golden—one of "better mettle."]

*The Gypsies Metamorphosed* (3, 5 Aug. and Sept. 1621)

**470**    FURNISS, W. Todd. "Ben Jonson's Masques." *Three Studies in the Renaissance: Sidney, Jonson, Milton.* New Haven: Yale Univ. Press, 1958. Pp. 141-51. ["The unity of the masque is a poetic unity" (p. 151) is an exact statement: in speeches to the king, nobles, and rustics, and gypsies' shifts in verse patterns betoken hierarchical and tonal distinctions.]

**471**    *RANDALL, Dale B.J. *Jonson's Gypsies Unmasked: Background and Theme in "The Gypsies Metamorphos'd."* Durham, NC: Duke Univ. Press, 1975. Pp. 67-176 et passim. [One of Jonson's most important masques is given a replete appraisal of its historico-sociological milieu in addition to its thematic, symbolic, and theatrical dimensions.]

*Hymenaei* (5 Jan. 1606)

**472**    *GORDON, D.J. *"Hymenaei:* Ben Jonson's Masque of Union." *JWCI,* 8 (1945), 107-45. [Universal union is symbolized in the dynastic marriage of Frances Howard to the Earl of Essex. Jonson's considerable learning, realized through the use of decor (the microcosmic globe), music, movement, and costume as emblematic metaphor, is fully documented.]

---

Notes and Additions

## Love Restored (6 Jan. 1612)

473    *BARISH, Jonas A. *Ben Jonson and the Language of Prose Comedy.* Cambridge, MA: Harvard Univ. Press, 1960. Pp. 251-60. [Several formal innovations emerge now in response to Jonson's bent toward realism: satiric comic prose, entire suppression of the antimasque (by Plutus in a double role), and self-reflexive comment upon the masque genre itself.]

474    ORGEL, Stephen. *The Jonsonian Masque.* Cambridge, MA: Harvard Univ. Press, 1965. Pp. 72-77. [Princes need love *and* riches: "Cupid's defeat of Plutus is a justification of both liberality and masquing; after the deception of the antimasque of riches, the masque of love represents a symbolic vision of the virtues of the court and its king" (p. 74).]

## Love's Welcome at Bolsover (30 July 1634)

475    FURNISS, W. Todd. "Ben Jonson's Masques." *Three Studies in the Renaissance: Sidney, Jonson, Milton.* New Haven: Yale Univ. Press, 1958. Pp. 164-67. [In the course of Philalethes' final speech (ll. 159-90), Jonson shifts the central symbols from Eros and Anteros (Love and Love-again) to King Charles and Queen Henrietta Maria as ideal love and union.]

## The Masque at Lord Haddington's Marriage (9 Feb. 1608)

476    *GORDON, D.J. "Ben Jonson's *Haddington Masque:* the Story and the Fable." *MLR,* 42 (1947), 180-87. [Central to this masque is the idea, symbolized by the celestial globe and the zodiacal circle, that marriage is the *perfection* of life. The fable concerns marital procreation, which needs heat (Vulcan) and desire (Venus) in order to be fulfilled.]

477    MEAGHER, John C. *Method and Meaning in Jonson's Masques.* Notre Dame, IN: Notre Dame Univ. Press, 1966. Pp. 133-36. [Cupid and his train represent a disordered love which, when subsumed

into the discipline of marriage, achieves a perfected, total harmony. Love's qualified triumph is realized scenographically in the emblematic decor, and musically.]

## The Masque of Beauty (10 Jan. 1608)

**478**    *GORDON, D.J. "The Imagery of Ben Jonson's *The Masque of Blacknesse* and *The Masque of Beautie.*" *JWCI*, 6 (1943), 122-41. [Using mythographies and emblem books, Gordon explains the central image, the Throne of Beauty, as "a translation into visual terms of certain ideas about love and beauty held by Ficino and the Florentine Platonists" (p. 130).]

## The Masque of Blackness (6 Jan. 1605)

**479**    *GORDON, D.J. "The Imagery of Ben Jonson's *The Masque of Blacknesse* and *The Masque of Beautie.*" *JWCI*, 6 (1943), 122-41. [Jonson drew upon Giovanni Valeriano's *Hieroglyphica* (1595) to create the twelve Ethiopian nymphs for impersonation by the Queen and her companions. The hieroglyphs give thematic emphasis to the tempering òf heat by cold.]

**480**    ORGEL, Stephen. *The Jonsonian Masque.* Cambridge, MA: Harvard Univ. Press, 1965. Pp. 113-28. [Music and dancing were primary elements in Elizabethan masques, and a contemporary termed Jonson's first effort a "pagent" because of its novel theatricality. Blackness, which is paradoxical beauty, comprises a symbolic antimasque within the masque.]

**481**    MEAGHER, John C. *Method and Meaning in Jonson's Masques.* Notre Dame, IN: Notre Dame Univ. Press, 1966. Pp. 107-12. [Light is used metaphorically in many Jonsonian masques to signify kinds of perfection or value, but never so fully as here: the black-beauty paradox arises from Neoplatonic symbolism, by which light (sun=James I) can be beauty's judge.]

## The Masque of Queens (2 Feb. 1608)

**482**    *ORGEL, Stephen. *The Jonsonian Masque.* Cambridge, MA:
Harvard Univ. Press, 1965. Pp. 129-46. [Absolute good and evil (the
queens and the hags) do not interact in Jonson's Platonic universe,
but occupy discrete, antithetical sections of the masque until
mediated by a climactic scene shift. Theatrical and rhetorical data
share in the interpretation.]

**483**    *MEAGHER, John C. *Method and Meaning in Jonson's Masques.*
Notre Dame, IN: Notre Dame Univ. Press, 1966. Pp. 152-57.
[Mindful of the Romans' known attachment to triumphs, Jonson,
in a masque expressing the relationship of virtue to fame,
appropriately uses music and spectacle of the triumph form to
celebrate the Queens' vanquishing the hags of Anti-Fame.]

*Mercury Vindicated from the Alchemists at Court* (1 Jan. 1616)

**484**    *DUNCAN, Edgar Hill. "The Alchemy is Jonson's *Mercury
Vindicated." SP,* 39 (1943), 625-37. [For both the conception and for
visual and verbal details of the antimasque Jonson's indebtedness
to Paracelsus and other alchemic writers is large. Two ideas come
under satiric attack: that nature is in decay and that nature is
alchemy's inferior competitor.]

**485**    *BARISH, Jonas A. *Ben Jonson and the Language of Prose
Comedy.* Cambridge, MA: Harvard Univ. Press, 1960. Pp. 261-66.
[Jonson "improvises a brilliant mock myth that allows him to move
simultaneously on several thematic levels" (p. 261) by making
alchemy an object of satire and a metaphor for false art. The king
(as Sol) redeems decayed Nature.]

*Neptune's Triumph for the Return of Albion* (6 Jan. 1624)

**486**    FURNISS, W. Todd. "Ben Jonson's Masques." *Three Studies in the
Renaissance: Sidney, Jonson, Milton.* New Haven: Yale Univ.
Press, 1958. Pp. 152-58. [Pages 152-56 distinguish the masque from
others of Jonson's efforts in the "triumph" group, after which the
function of symbolic spectacle to express King James I's

(Neptune's) magnificence is noted.]

**487**   *ORGEL, Stephen. *The Jonsonian Masque.* Cambridge, MA: Harvard Univ. Press, 1965. Pp. 91-99. [More than "rival show," the cook's antimasque and the poet's masque are organically related and complementary sections; the former allegorizes the courtly "relish" for rumor and untruth, while the latter truly mythicizes Prince Charles's Spanish voyage.]

## *Oberon, the Fairy Prince* (1 Jan. 1611)

**488**   *ORGEL, Stephen. *The Jonsonian Masque.* Cambridge, MA: Harvard Univ. Press, 1965. Pp. 81-91. [Moral transformation is imaged not instantly, as in the earlier *Masque of Queens,* but in a more gradual shift from antimasque to masque: chaos and indecorum of the satyrs' world give way to the music, pageantry, courtliness, grace, and order of Oberon's.]

**489**   FULLER, David. "The Jonsonian Masque and Its Music." *M&L,* 54 (1973), 440-52. [Masque and antimasque, the two structural sections, are not musically differentiated by melody, harmony, or rhythm, but rather through scoring, which permits instrumental groups and tone-colors to represent aurally the symbolic contrast between satyrs and fairy knights.]

## *Pan's Anniversary* (19 June 1620)

**490**   *FURNISS, W. Todd. "Ben Jonson's Masques." *Three Studies in the Renaissance: Sidney, Jonson, Milton.* New Haven: Yale Univ. Press, 1958. Pp. 128-37. [In the main masque, Arcadians dance and sing quasi-liturgical humns in ritual praise of James I (Pan) as fertility god; in the antimasque, there are influences of Roman and English folk fertility rites.]

## *Pleasure Reconciled to Virtue* (6 Jan. 1618)

**491**   *FURNISS, W. Todd. "Ben Jonson's Masques." *Three Studies in the*

*Renaissance: Sidney, Jonson, Milton.* New Haven: Yale Univ. Press, 1958. Pp. 169-76. [By the king's presence as the star, Hesperus, about whose throne stands a constellation of virtues, the masque takes on cosmic meaning when the dancers symbolically negotiate Daedalus' ethical labyrinth.]

492    *ORGEL, Stephen. *The Jonsonian Masque.* Cambridge, MA: Harvard Univ. Press, 1965. Pp. 147-85. [With this example, Jonson completes making the masque "very nearly self-sufficient as a work of literature. Even its dances become poetry" (p. 151). Focuses upon iconography, stylistics, the two antimasques, and the final aural-visual display of *wisdom.*]

493    *PETERSON, Richard S. "The Iconography of Jonson's *Pleasure Reconciled to Virtue." JMRS,* 5 (1975), 123-62. [A full thematic explication of the masque in light of the emblematic and mythographic traditions of its visual motifs: the revelry of Comus, Bacchus' procession, the choice of Hercules, Hercules' ambiguous reclining, Theseus' maze, etc.]

## Prince Henry's Barriers (6 Jan. 1610)

494    FURNISS, W. Todd. "Ben Jonson's Masques." *Three Studies in the Renaissance: Sidney, Jonson, Milton.* New Haven: Yale Univ. Press, 1958. Pp. 124-27. [Jonson inverts the central aim of the barriers, a martial entertainment celebrating battle prowess, by having Merlin interpret a heraldic shield so as to praise James I as a peace-maker and cosmic unifier.]

## Time Vindicated to Himself and to His Honors (19 Jan. 1623)

495    *FURNISS, W. Todd. "Ben Jonson's Masques." *Three Studies in the Renaissance: Sidney, Jonson, Milton.* New Haven: Yale Univ. Press, 1958. Pp. 109-19. [Unity in both masque and antimasque sections is achieved by the imagery of time. Central symbol is the Golden Age myth, whereby King James is equated with Saturn, god of the Age, and the Lord of Time.]

*The Vision of Delight* (6 Jan. 1617)

**496**    *HAWKINS, Harriett. "Jonson's Use of Traditional Dream Theory in *The Vision of Delight.*" *MP,* 64 (1967), 285-92. [By using as his framework the various types of dreams (the *oraculum, visio,* etc.) classified in Macrobius' *In Somnium Scipionis,* Jonson gives symbolic force to King James' climactic appearance, as though in fulfillment of an oracular dream.]

# THOMAS MIDDLETON

*The Triumphs of Truth* (29 Oct. 1613)

**497**    *BERGERON, David M. *English Civic Pageantry 1558-1642.* Columbia: Univ. of South Carolina Press, 1971. Pp. 179-86. [With an unsurpassed understanding of traditional allegorical iconography, Middleton has Truth and Error's struggle take the morality play's form. As a symbolic structure, the clash of light and darkness emerges in word and spectacle.]

# JOHN MILTON (1608-1674)

*Arcades* (fragment; 1630-1634)

**498**    BROOKS, Cleanth, and John Edward HARDY. *Poems of Mr. John Milton: The 1645 Edition with Essays in Analysis.* New York: Harcourt, 1951. Pp. 163-68. [Celebrates Britain as the new homeland of Arcadian pastoral poetry, with the Countess Dowager, to whom Spenser her cousin had dedicated *Tears of the Muses,* as its patroness, spirit, and presiding deity.]

**499**    *WALLACE, John Malcolm. "Milton's *Arcades.*" *JEGP,* 58 (1959), 627-36. [Central symbol is the near-mythological figure of the famed patroness of learning and *Arcades'* honoree, the Dowager Countess herself, here personfied as a Christianized goddess of sapience through comparisons to Latona, Cybele, and the wise Solomon, host to an admiring Queen of Sheba.]

**500**  *DEMARAY, John G. *"Arcades* as a Literary Entertainment." *PLL,* 8 (1972), 15-26. [Symbolic action at the conclusion of *Arcades* as an enacted entertainment resolves the tension between the disordered, fatalistic pagan world (embodied in Arcadian disguise) and the actual, redeemed Christian world at Harefield, personified in the matriarchal Lady Alice.]

*Comus* (29 Sept. 1634)

**501**  *WOODHOUSE, A.S.P. "The Argument of Milton's *Comus.*" *UTQ,* 11 (1941), 46-71. [This classic, influential study describes the two existential levels at issue in temperance-continence-chastity-virginity, and reconciled in *Comus:* the orders of nature (the physical world, and man's rational ethics) and grace (God's law, received by religious faith).]

**502**  *BROOKS, Cleanth, and John Edward HARDY. *Poems of Mr. John Milton: The 1645 Edition with Essays in Analysis.* New York: Harcourt, 1951. Pp. 187-237. [By Hardy actually, this essay is a fine example of the New Criticism, with its focus upon character in relation to Christian/pagan symbolism and dialectical image patterns—light and darkness especially.]

**503**  TUVE, Rosemond. *Images & Themes in Five Poems by Milton.* Cambridge, MA: Harvard Univ. Press, 1957. Pp. 112-61. [Among the first to treat *Comus* generically, Tuve propounds the historicist's view of tropological decorum in Milton's symbolical/allegorical images: pastoralism, light and dark, the Circe myth. They are inseparably Christian and pagan.]

**504**  *WILKENFELD, Roger B. "The Seat at the Center: An Interpretation of *Comus.*" *ELH,* 33 (1966), 170-97. [Wilkenfeld's style is distracting at times, but his correlations of theme (freedom and constraint, transformation), and presentation (sitting, rising, dancing figures) are most fitting.]

505   *NEUSE, Richard. "Metamorphosis and Symbolic Action in *Comus." ELH,* 34 (1967), 49-64. [Metamorphosis is a broadly functional concept: in haemony, once a flower but now a divinely efficacious root; in the Spirit, embodied in the mortal Thyrsis; in Sabrina, symbolizing spirit-infused nature; and in the masque functioning as mythopoeic social ritual.]

506   *BOYETTE, Purvis E. "Milton's Abstracted Sublimities: The Structure of Meaning in *A Mask." TSE,* 18 (1970), 35-58. [A richly allusive explication of both the literal and metaphoric meanings of settings and characters. Theatrical symbolism and the emblematic tradition behind the pilgrimage-of-life and choice-of-life themes are particularized.]

507   SHAW, Catherine M. "The Unity of *Comus." XUS,* 10 (1971), 33-43. [Milton advances the Court Masque by infusing its formal conventions—songs, the debate, masque and antimasque dances— with the drama's unifying capabilities of theme and structure, and by enhancing the symbolic impact of *Comus'* lighting effects, scenic devices, songs and stage grouping.]

# SIR PHILIP SIDNEY (1554-1586)

*The Lady of May* (1578-1582)

508   ORGEL, S.K. "Sidney's Experiment in Pastoral: *The Lady of May." JWCI,* 26 (1963), 198-203. [At issue is the familiar antithesis of the pastoral mode, the active versus the contemplative life, which Sidney's masquers examine in a series of debates that give forensic advantage to Therion's activist position—but the Queen renders an unexpected judgment.]

**509**    *PICKETT, Penny. "Sidney's Use of *Phaedrus* in *The Lady of May.*" *SEL*, 16 (1976), 33-50. [No "masque" or "entertainment"—rather, the work is a full-fledged Platonic poem that draws upon Plato's *Phaedrus* metaphor of the charioteer (May Lady) drawn by mild and wild horses (Espilus, Therion) to allegorize action and passivity as unreconciled contraries.]

# JOHN TAYLOR (1580-1653)

*The Triumphs of Fame and Honour* (29 Oct. 1634)

**510**    WILLIAMS, Sheila. "A Lord Mayor's Show by John Taylor, the Water Poet." *BJRL*, 41 (1959), 501-31. [Closely examines Taylor's major achievement as a pageant poet—its allegorical and mythological personages, processions by land and water, the imagery and actions of its five segments. An illuminating essay on this unique genre of popular entertainment.]

# ANONYMOUS

*Time's Distractions* (M. Fane? G. Chapman?; Sep. 1642-5 Aug. 1643)

**511**    *STROMMER, Diane Weltner, ed. *Time's Distractions: A Play from the Time of Charles I.* College Station: Texas A&M Univ. Press, 1976. Pp. 11-39. [Strommer terms a play what others more reasonably call a pastoral-allegorical entertainment, but that is to cavil about an otherwise valuable assessment of the moral, socio-political, mythic, and visual symbolisms.]

# Index of Authors

# Analytical Subject Index

**Disguise** *(continued)*

as bellman 435 439
as bumpkin: lost innocence 428
as canon lawyer: change of nature 179
as citizen's wife: by a prostitute 90
as corpse: a life-affirming act 377
as courtesan: comic amorality 370
as courtesan: prurient eroticism 365
as courtier: sign of effeteness 99
as Cupid: by Plutus (=wealth) 473-74
deception, for purposes of 276 368
devil as woman 370
as a divine: change of nature 179
as female warrior: male cowardice 301
as a fool: ironic transformation 304
as gypsies: embodiments of fraud 471
as gypsies: a penitential existence 381
as king: paradoxical reality 38
as madmen: symbolic "changes" 346
as madwoman 87
as malcontent 314 316
master/fool exchange: misrule 130-31
as means of festive clarification 100
multiple disguises: connoting wit 359
    366
multiple disguises: moral changes 225
multiple disguises: moral unfixedness
    359
as noblewoman: by one worthy/un-
    worthy 199
as old Irish nurse: hidden ideal 198
prince in fool's dress: as ironic 132
prince/fool exhange: psychic symbol 134
as royal subject: learning-process 379
as a scholar: psychic symbolism 106
as a shepherd: false status 248 506
as a shoemaker: class vitality 96
as a shoemaker: humility 99
as a shoemaker: social acceptance 98
as sick man: moral reality 225
as sign of ethical change 311 422
as sign of evaded guilt 438
as sign of ineffectuality 301
as sign of lost identity 382
as sign of low fortune 52
as sign of misleading appearances 28
as sign of "role-playing" 320
social reform, for purposes of 89 309
    377
as tomb-maker 439
"virtues" personated by "vices" 172
witch disguised as her enemy 207
*see also* Costume
*Doctor Faustus* 263-69
concordance to 15

*Downfall of Robert, Earl of Huntington,
    The* 396
Dream theory, Renaissance 245 496; *see
    also* Themes: dream-vision
*Duchess of Malfi, The* 434-40
figurative language, index to 20
Duelling code, Renaissance 353
*Duke of Milan, The* 331
Dumbshow, *see* Structure
*Dutch Courtesan, The* 307-09

*Eastward Ho* 62-65
*Edward II* 270-76
concordance to 15
*Edward III* 454
concordance to 15
*1 & 2 Edward IV*
figurative language, index to 12
Edwards, Richard: as influence 260
*Elvetham, The Entertainment at* 461
Emblematic staging 9 48 69 125 151-52 164
    172 235 240 259-60 265 276 280 282 292
    299 304 398 402-03 406 418 428 437 464
    477 497 504 506
**Emblems, thematically significant**
Actaeon: as sensualist 276
adder (cf. serpent) 245
Aeneas carrying Anchises 163
archer aims at crane: human pride 245
ass: connoting miserliness 282
Ate: discord personified 162
Bacchus' procession 493
Beauty 478
Bethsabe in the bath 405-06
Caprice 462
cauldron, boiling 277 282
Comus (cf. Comus' revelry) 492-93
crane, *see* archer 245
Cupid defeated by Anteros (=virtue) 172
Desidia (=sloth), *see* Sloth
Despair 267
Diana & Endymion: releasing love 245
eagle: as self-protectiveness 73
Fortune 318 463
Four Virgins: symbol of mercy 292
Harmony 478
hell-mouth 151
Hercules: as heroic virtue 69
Hercules & Antaeus 493
Hercules' choice (Virtue or Vice) 492-93
    506
Hercules' reclining 493
hieroglyphs, Renaissance 479
Ira (= wrath) 133